FINDING PURPOSE IN HIS WORD
VOLUME 2

(A 30-DAY JOURNEY OF SPIRITUAL INSPIRATION)

Linda Peat Israel

authorHOUSE

AuthorHouse™
1663 Liberty Drive
Bloomington, IN 47403
www.authorhouse.com
Phone: 833-262-8899

Published by AuthorHouse 11/08/2021

ISBN: 978-1-6655-4323-1 (sc)
ISBN: 978-1-6655-4327-9 (e)

Library of Congress Control Number: 2021922616

Contents

Contents

Acknowledgements

My closest friend approached me one day and told me that the Lord had placed in her spirit to begin a daily devotional entitled, "A Word In Due Season" which would be sent to email subscribers on a daily basis during the work week. She also said He had put it upon her heart to add contributing writers to assist her with writing these devotionals, and after praying, my name came up.

Initially, I wanted to tell her...God gave this to you and not me... so you go forth in the power of His might! But somehow the Holy Spirit would not allow me to do that, and so upon accepting, I began writing with her in 2006. It was then I realized that what God was giving me to pen was actually ministering into the lives of others. So I thank God for my girlfriend, La Kesha Ford Calhoun, for being obedient to the Holy Spirit's leading and pulling this book out of me, which is a product of the daily inspirational devotions. I love you girlfriend and sister!

I want to thank my parents, Robert (now deceased) & Willie Mae Peat, for raising me with morals, values, and integrity. Thank you for training me up in the way that I should go...as you can see, although I strayed, I knew how to come back. I love you all so very much and thank God for having you as parents.

To the best children in the whole wide world. We've have been through a lot...more than many know, but we have learned that God has not failed us nor has He forsaken us. He's always made a way for us when we needed Him and for that we are eternally grateful! I love you Brittney Danielle, Kaitlyn Ashley, and Victor Lowery Middlebrook (Lauren). You all have made me a proud mother and I love you more than you can fathom. Keep your heads up and remain focused. God has great things in store for each of you and I can't wait to see His plans for you come to life before my very eyes!

To my grands who have given me a renewed passion for life, Emmanuel, Malachi, and Avaeah…you make Nana's heart smile every time I hear you call my name. My prayer for each of you is that you find "Your Purpose" in this life and you do everything you were designed to do! Make the world proud of you just as I am!

Preface

Within the pages of "Volume 2 - *Finding Purpose in His Word: A 30 Day Journey of Spiritual Inspiration*" are true stories and testimonials, which have been shared with thousands across the world. These testimonials and God inspired writings have touched the lives of many and have caused deliverance in the lives of its readers.

This book is the product of a daily email devotional, created for readers from the database of "A Word In Due Season Ministries," of which La Kesha Ford Calhoun is the founder, and I have been a contributing writer since 2006. Wow! Look at God! If it had not been for this great Woman of God, my dear friend, my Sister in Christ, my Blood Sister because we both have the same father; our daddy and Abba Father God...this book would not be in circulation! She pushed me when I didn't feel like writing; and when the Holy Spirit was inspiring me, she would call and say..."I'm not getting anything today, can you write?"

What you need to know most of all is that I share from the heart because God has challenged me to be transparent. I've learned over the years that transparency is the opening of the heart, and what comes from the heart, reaches the heart. If God keeps me and delivers me through the experience, then I have an obligation to tell it! I love God too much and know that I am only here because of His Grace and Mercy. Without it...literally I would be six feet under... and that alone is a testimony!

Endorsements

"Thy word is a lamp unto my feet and a light unto my path." Psalms 119:105. Brilliantly, spotlighted by Linda in her spirit led compilation *Finding Purpose in His Word*. Linda has provided us with a lamp and the light of God's word is shining brightly on this journey.

This book takes us on a journey of trust in Jesus and following in His footsteps. As this helps our path become easier to see. Living in this dark world, the light of His word is needed more now than ever before. This book *Finding Purpose in His Word* compiles Linda's discernment of scriptural references and testimonials of how the word of God works that provides inspiration, hope, light and instruction. This book has blessed my soul and "lit" my spirit and it will do the same for you. This book is a must read.

–**Supervisor Mary Tucker**
Supervisor of Women North Central GA COGIC
McDonough, GA

Linda Peat Israel is an anointed vessel of God who uses her life experiences to pull on the heart strings of her reading audience. She doesn't shy away from her past and encourages others to live "beyond" theirs as well. In her latest book, *Finding Purpose in His Word*, she challenges readers to navigate life's challenges by finding healing, hope, strength, and purpose in His Word.

I am certain that once you pick up the book, you will not be able to put it down. Ask me how I know? Because neither could I. May each word you read, each page your turn, bring you closer to finding your purpose in His Word. Because guess what? We all have one, and this book has been anointed by God to help you find yours!

–**La'Kesha Ford Calhoun**
First Lady, Greater Somerville Church,
Memphis, TN

Powerful!!! Genuine and Authentic!!
Reviewed in the United States on October 15, 2021
Verified Purchase - Volume One

This book is changing my life. It is so authentically written and rooted in scripture! I am so thankful to have this book in my life and I am now walking in expectancy of the great blessings God has in store for me!

–D.M. Williams
Hope Mills, NC

Are You Prepared for Your Blessing?

Then he said, "Go, borrow thee vessels abroad of all thy neighbors, even empty vessels; borrow not a few. And when thou art come in, thou shalt shut the door upon thee and upon thy sons, and shalt pour out into all those vessels, and thou shalt set aside that which is full." So she went from him, and shut the door upon her and upon her sons, who brought the vessels to her; and she poured out. And it came to pass, when the vessels were full, that she said unto her son, Bring me yet a vessel. And he said unto her, *there is not a vessel more?* And the oil stayed. – 2 Kings 4:3-6 KJV

This is indeed the season of New Beginnings and I believe God is getting ready to do some awesome and mighty things in the lives of His people. However, I have a question for you today: Are you prepared for your blessing? I mean, are you really and truly prepared for your blessing? Are you prepared for that which God is getting ready to do in your life? If you had one thing you really wanted God to do for you...what would that one thing be? Now that you have that thing in your mind...ask yourself if you are ready to receive it. I asked that simple question to get you in the place of checking our faith. How is your faith today? Has God ever shown Himself faithful to you in a way that you knew it was no one but God?

When we look at the above passage of scripture, we have a widowed mother who really loves her sons. She was poor...broke, busted and disgusted. She was about to lose her sons to slavery because she could not pay her debts. BUT GOD! He sent the Prophet Elisha the widow woman's way. When the Prophet asked what she had in her house... she told him, "nothing, BUT a pot of oil." Therefore, he asked her to go out and borrow some vessels. There are four (4) important words in this scripture that were instrumental to purpose: "BORROW NOT A FEW." He then told her to close themselves up (herself and her sons) and pour into the vessels. As she began to pour into all the vessels they had collected...she asked for another and there was

1

none. Why…Because they borrowed only a few. In other words, the number of vessels they collected was representation of their faith. My theory is, they were looking or measuring with their eyes, and so in their mind, there was no way that the little pot of oil could fill up a large number of vessels. It is right here they were limiting their faith AND their blessing. Keep in mind, as long as there was a vessel to pour into, there was oil…but when they ran out of vessels… the oil stopped coming. Read the above passage again. If that had been me…and I realized WHO was commanding me, I would have knocked on every door in the neighborhood, then walked down the street to the next neighborhood, AND went across town knocking on every door.

It is true that God can do exceeding, abundantly above all that we ask or THINK…**BUT it is according to the power that works in us.** (Ephesians 3:20 KJV) So, are you really prepared for your blessing? God's "PROVISION" is as large as your faith and willingness to obey Him when He speaks. If we aren't obedient to His word… how can we be ready for His blessings? First, we have to hear Him with a spiritual ear. Had the widow woman and her sons heard the prophet with a spiritual ear…they wouldn't have missed out on the "abundant" blessing God had already made provision for. If they had heard with a spiritual ear, their faith would have been greater than the few bottles they collected. Yes they did receive plenty, but just think how much more they would have received…and how long the oil would have lasted had their faith been greater. The more bottles, the more oil. One person might say that this is being greedy, but in essence it is not. Why not, you say? Because when God is ready to bless you, He is the one who determines the size of your blessing and we are the ones who can limit the blessing. Do you remember the Word that God declared in Malachi 3:10 KJV that He will open up the windows of heaven and pour you out a blessing that you don't have room enough to receive? In essence, the widow woman didn't even have the room to receive the blessing...no more bottles to pour into. Remember, the oil didn't stop coming until they didn't have any more bottles to pour into.

In order to be ready for our blessings, we must know what God is saying to us when He speaks. By studying His word, fasting, praying, being obedient, listening with a spiritual ear...we can be tuned in to His channel and know how to be ready when the blessing comes. If we are ready, we won't miss out on the abundant blessing He has made provision for. Get ready now...because I'm going to prophecy in the Spirit...someone who is reading this word today is about to come into a 100 fold blessing. I hear God speaking in my Spirit that it will be an unmistakable blessing. Because He makes no mistakes. When He does this thing in your life...you are going to have to run and I mean run for Him. This blessing WILL overtake you and the people won't be able to say that man did it...I DID IT, says the Lord! Don't be afraid to share what I did...How can I get the Glory when the people don't know what I did? I am a jealous God...and man does not deserve the credit for what I am getting ready to do...I won't have it. Now get ready, get in tune and watch God overtake you with His blessings.

Go and Get Your Inheritance!

And I will restore to you the years that the locust hath eaten, the cankerworm, and the caterpillar, and the palmerworm, my great army which I sent among you. And ye shall eat in plenty, and be satisfied, and praise the name of the Lord your God, that hath dealt wondrously with you: and my people shall never be ashamed. Joel 2:25-26 KJV

I had received a prophetic word that frightened the living daylights out of me. Scared me so much so that I wanted to run and hide…one that I thought, certainly this person is off…God won't allow this… would He? What would you do if someone came to you today and boldly said: "Sister/Brother, the Lord says that He is going to strip you of everything that you have." What would your reaction be? If you have gone through or going through a dry season in your life… let me share a portion of my testimony with you today. It may seem long…but please bear with me because purpose is tied to it.

I was one of those people who experienced a desolate prophecy. This thing scared me because I personally knew the prophetess who was speaking into my life. I knew the words that God had spoken through her in times past had come to pass. At first, I didn't understand why He would allow this to happen to me, but again, as time passed, I began to understand it by and by…as the old folks used to say. God wanted to strip me of the old man…of my old ways…of all the ways that wasn't like Him, so that He could prepare me for the new things He had laid up for me. Oh yeah, God has some stuff He wants to give us before we leave this earth…but we have to get rid of some things. And when we can't do it on our own, He sends the locusts and the cankerworm to eat up that stuff He wants to shed us of. Sometimes restoration can take months; sometimes it can take years, but how we react to what He is doing in our lives will determine the outcome. He knows just how long He wants to take. With me, He gave me a five year dry season. Now for someone else, it might take longer or it could be shorter. This was my season.

Little by little, the cankerworm ate up everything I possessed…right down to the roof over my head. At the time I became homeless, God graced me to be able to send my children away for the summer, so they would not have to suffer living in extended stay hotels or staying in strange people's homes I was keeping while they were away; just to have a bed to sleep in. It wasn't meant for them…it was meant for me. I took it all in stride and kept remembering that this had to happen, but Romans 8:28 stayed with me, "And we know that all things work together for good to them that love God, to them who are the called according to his purpose." So I continued to believe that He would bring me out. God allowed me to get approved to purchase a home, but my contract expired and someone came along and bought the house out from under me. I thought…ok, God you must have something better for me. So I kept looking…nothing surfaced. It was time to put the children back into school and I had not established residence. I was blessed to find a house somewhat like the one I was going to buy, but on a lease to purchase option. I took it! To God be the Glory!

When it came time to buy the home, I didn't feel it in my spirit, and I told the owner that I would let him know when I was ready. While getting ready for church one Sunday, my son, who was only 5 years old at the time, said to me: Momma, you are going to get married again. I was curling my hair and so it stopped me dead in my tracks. I thought, how would a five-year-old even know what this mean. I said to him, "and how do you know this;" and He said, "Because I know." In the back of my mind, I was thinking surely God didn't show him my dream from the night before…or was I talking in my sleep? I had dreamt that my husband was waiting for me at the altar. In my mind, I knew specific features about my husband, so all I could do was wait.

Not long afterwards, I met a gentleman who was kind, generous, loving, handsome, and God fearing. He was a believer, and while that wasn't all I wanted or needed in a mate; it was enough for this season. Besides…I didn't have a clue…I set my standards and he met them all. After a very short courtship, we were married. I watched God bless our union in a tremendous way. Not only did my deal to purchase a home fall through, but before I met my husband, his deal to purchase a home fell through and he ended up stuck in his apartment until the day we met and then married…but there was purpose behind all of that.

One day we sat down and decided we would work on our credit to get into position to purchase a home. We started paying off our bills one by one. We started going to an agency that helps you rebuild your credit and also finance you for a home…but they had a lengthy process. We began looking for an existing home around the amount they would finance us for, which was their maximum. The very same prophetess that spoke desolation over my life came back and began to speak prosperity. She began to minister to me and told me that the Lord said, "we would not compromise when we purchase our FIRST home, we could have what we want." And that…"We will have a brand new 5 bedroom or more home and we will not have to settle for anything less." So I began to share this with my husband and we just believed God. One day after getting off from work, I began to drive around looking at homes and areas to live. I was on my way to find a particular house when I passed by a new subdivision. I was nudged to turn into the subdivision. I got out and looked around. Went home, cooked dinner then took my daughter back because I wanted her to see it. We went into the only home that was FINISHED. We began walking around counting the rooms. We went from one end to the next…and then I called my husband and told him that we had a subdivision we wanted him to see.

That weekend we all went. As he was walking through the house, he turned to me and said, "Honey…this feels like home." I said back to him, "it sure does, doesn't it." Our hearts were fixed, our minds were made up…and we began to take possession of the house. Every day, we drove over there and staked our claim. The word was going forth over the pulpit through our then Pastor and we were grabbing hold of that word. We continued to go by, anointing the door knobs, pouring blessed oil on the concrete around the perimeter, claiming what God had saved for us. We went to a different lender...got the financing but didn't like the interest rate. My husband heard the Lord say "WAIT," and so we said NO, God's blessing does not bring with it sorrow. We would not have been able to live on what was left after their intended house note for us. We met a young lady who referred us to another lender. And just light that...they came back with a much better interest rate which brought our house payment within reach!! We knew the favor of God was upon us. We gave them $1,000 in earnest money to secure the home, then another $250 for the appraisal. They gave us a closing date.

Now...I don't know about you...but I serve a B-I-G God and He knows just how to bless His people. I called the lender and asked them how much money we would need to bring to the closing because we didn't want to get there and be surprised. I could hear her punching the calculator over the phone...then she came back with $516.00 or so. I called my husband and told him to be prepared to withdraw from our savings. We then got a call from the lender with a closing date and time. I asked for a definitive amount to close. She said, "You don't have to bring any more money to close; as a matter of fact, you are going to be getting your $1,000 back when you get here." I was at work of course so I couldn't scream...but I said shut yo mouth...watchu say?? I said never mind...THANK YOU GOD!!! You see, that is the God that I serve...a BIG God who is blessing in BIG ways!!

We closed on our 5 bedroom, 3 ½ bath home!!!! HALLALUJAH... THANK YOU JESUS!!! I heard a preacher once say that the Lord told him that this was the year for VICTORY, ACCESS, and OWNERSHIP! Which of the three do you want? You don't have to settle for one... you can have them all. Even now God is blessing his people with beautiful homes, and if you are one of those waiting on God to manifest Himself to you...get in the place where you can hear Him. He is speaking...He is leading...He is guiding...but don't move until He tells you to move. "At the Lord's command they encamped, and at the Lord's command they set out. They obeyed the Lords order, in accordance with His command through Moses." (Numbers 9:23) I didn't have the best credit...as a matter of fact...I'm a 3-time bankruptcy filer with numerous evictions...somebody say, BUT GOD! He has some things laid up for you that no man can touch... not even your haters!! Pay your tithes and your offerings...commit to the ways of God, then watch God show mercy in your situation. God said that He will open up a window FROM Heaven and pour you out a blessing that you won't have room enough to receive. One final note I must add. We needed to purchase a refrigerator...that is why the Lord gave us back the $1,000... so that we could go and pay cash for it and not have to open up additional credit! Isn't God Good?! I will answer that...YES he is!!

You may not be one who's believing God for a new home...it may be a new car, a new job or promotion on the one you have, restoration in your marriage, a breakthrough in your finances, deliverance for your children or family members; but whatever it is, may my testimony encourage you that God can do exceedingly, abundantly above all you ask or think (Ephesians 3:20 KJV). Even when man says you can't have it...if God says you can...then it's yours! So man of God, woman of God...take the limits off of God. He can do all that you're believing Him for AND more. But you have to be in position to receive. And if you are...then I dare you to go and take possession of what God has for you! After all, it's your inheritance!

Let God Be What You Need Him to Be

Commit thy way unto the Lord, trust also in Him, and He shall bring it to pass. - Psalm 37:5 KJV

If I asked you the question, "Who is God to you," what would your answer be? I want you to let that question marinate on your mind for a moment. Someone might confess like David did in Psalms 40:17 KJV, "Thou are my **help** AND my **deliverer**." There is no doubt God was David's present help in the time of trouble, especially when he came up against the lion, the bear and even the giant, Goliath. Let's take it a little deeper than that because David knew that he was nothing without God. Psalms 40:2 KJV reads, "He brought me up also out of a horrible pit, out of the miry clay, and set my feet upon a rock, and established my goings." WHATCHU SAY David?!!! You better speak that thing!! That scripture made me think back on how God was my deliverer...my present help indeed! And when I began to think about this...I began to thank God all over again. I immediately thought back to the time I was about to plunge to my demise. As I was in the midst of plummeting to my death, I called on the name of Jesus to save me...and that is just what he did!! Hallelujah...Thank You Jesus!! How about you? I'm sure you can think of a time when God delivered you.

Another person might say that God is my healer, just like the woman with the issue of blood confesses. She had this issue for twelve long years. And she knew without a shadow of doubt that if she could just touch the hem of His garment, she WOULD be healed. Is He your healer? Someone else might call Him their "Way Maker" as the widow woman in 1st Kings 17th Chapter did when she didn't know how she would get the money to pay her bills. God sent His prophet to make the way for her. I can say there have been many times in my life when I didn't know where the next meal was coming from or how I would keep the utilities on. I serve a God who knows all of my needs and He has always shown up just in time to make the way for me.

Did I hear someone call Him a Friend? You can't ask for a better friend. He listens to you when no one else will. He watches your back when you are sleeping. He is always around when you need Him; and even when you don't know that you need Him, He's yet there. I can say that He is my shelter…my refuge…my protector. When the storms of life are raging and beating down on me, He has me covered. I read in the 7th Chapter of 2nd Kings KJV that He is a Provider. I know you can't ask them now, but the four leprous men could tell you that he is, because when they were starving…the good Lord provided food, water, AND some STUFF. Go back and read what they walked upon. Not only did God provide plenty for them, but He provided enough for them to share with others in the city!!!

These are just a few ways that people back in the day TRUSTED God and committed their ways unto Him. They let God be who they needed Him to be. And just like they did, we can too. Who do you need God to be right now? Do you need Him to be a Healer? What about a Deliverer or Way-maker? How about your Keeper or Miracle Worker? I dare you to get that thing in your mind and sincerely ask God to be what you need Him to be in your life. Go ahead…He's waiting on you this very minute to confess that thing to Him.

I want to share a brief testimony. Many years ago I broke up with my boyfriend whom I cared for a great deal. I was lonely, and I needed to be held. (I don't mind confessing…because I got delivered). I would cry myself to sleep at night because I wanted someone to hold me. My ex must have felt me, because that man would call me and asked if he could stop by and see me. My body was screaming YEEEEES, but my PROTECTOR AND COMFORTER was saying NOOOOOO! ☺ God was my Keeper…even when I didn't want to be kept!!! He began to kiss my tears away…He began to take the hurt away…He became just what I needed Him to be…my keeper when I wanted a lover. You today what you want God to be to you, then trust Him and let God be just what you need Him to be!

<u>Stop Complaining</u>

And *when* the people complained, it displeased the Lord; and the Lord heard it; and his anger was kindled; and the fire of the Lord burnt among them, and consumed them that were in the uttermost parts of the camp. And the people cried unto Moses; and when Moses prayed unto the Lord, the fire was quenched. Numbers 11:1-2 KJV

Now that you've read the title and the Scripture…there shouldn't be any doubt in your mind where this word is going today…YEP…we're going to deal with that complaining spirit. I have to…you know why? God told me to. When I sat down to study the background text the Lord dropped in my spirit, I couldn't do anything but say OUCH! I had a situation in which I allowed the spirit of complaining to literally take over my mouth and my mind. I didn't realize it until I was standing in a quiet place alone at work and I clearly heard the Lord speak, "STOP COMPLAINING." I had the audacity to put my hand to my chest and say, who…Me? Then I realized there was no one in the room BUT me…and obviously God. Then suddenly everything that I had been complaining about began to flood my mind. The worst part of it all is that I was complaining to different individuals who couldn't change one thing about the situation… people like my husband…my closest friend…even other co-workers.

Have you been there? Are you there now…in that constant state of complaining? It may be a situation on your job…or at home… maybe even at your place of worship…it could be a loved one you are complaining about…a fellow church member or just a co-worker; or is it your environment? Whatever your situation is…the Lord says, STOP COMPLAINING! As a matter of fact, I found out while reading this text that I should have been praying rather than complaining. From reading the entire 11th Chapter of Numbers, you will find that the people were in a constant state of complaining. They complained pretty much through to the 21st Chapter of Numbers, and their

11

complaints weren't all against mankind…they were also against their circumstances and situation. When they complained, they not only complained to one another, but they complained to Moses. Now what did Moses do? He turned around and complained to God.

The key message in all of this is…Moses knew who to go to. He didn't complain back to another person. He complained to the only one that could do something about the situation, and that was God. Now God's response to the Israelite's complaints wasn't too positive…He sent fire and destroyed thousands of them. WHAT YOU SAY?!!! You mean to tell me that God was that angry at the people for complaining that He felt the only way to shut them up was to burn them to death? OH MY LORD! It's hard, but it's true… read the book. In order for the Lord to pull back His wrath…Moses had to intercede for the folks. When he went to God…what was God's response to Moses? He responded to Moses positively, because Moses went about the situation the right way. He took his complaints to the only one who could do anything about the situation…GOD. As I began repenting and promising the Lord that I would stop complaining, the Serenity Prayer dropped into my spirit. As I began to recite it, I remembered how many times I've only repeated the first sentence of that prayer. The real significance and true meat of the prayer came later. As a matter of fact, let's take the time to pray the serenity prayer together.

"God, grant me the serenity to accept the things I cannot change; Courage to change the things I can; and WISDOM to know the difference. Living one day at a time; Enjoying one moment at a time; Accepting hardships as the pathway to peace; taking, as He (Jesus) did, this sinful world as it is, not as I would have it; trusting that He (Jesus) will make all things right if I surrender to His Will; that I may be reasonably happy in this life and supremely happy with Him forever in the next. AMEN!"

Now, do you see what I mean by saying the entire prayer and not just the first full sentence? The only thing we have the power to CHANGE is ourselves and our attitudes. Do you have the **courage** to change how you react to situations and circumstances in your life? We can stop complaining about things that we have no control over and trust that God will make all things right by giving it up to Him, or we can continue on living a life stressed out with the cares of this world and find ourselves in an asylum. So, just as God spoke these two words to me, I speak them to you today, "STOP COMPLAINING." God knows just how to handle everything that concerns you!! He had to let me know that this was not my battle! So my fight ended today...I've surrendered to His Will. Everything that comes against me, I will endure it as a good soldier...with a smile on my face and a thank you Jesus in my spirit. Trust in the Lord, with all thine heart and lean not unto thine own understanding; in all thy ways acknowledge Him, and He shall direct thy paths. (Proverbs 3:5-6 KJV).

Have You Looked in the Mirror Lately?

And why beholdest thou the mote that is in thy brother's eye, but considerest not the beam that is in thine own eye? Or wilt thou say to thy brother, Let me pull out the mote out of thine eye; and, behold, a beam is in thine own eye? – Matthew 7:3-4 KJV

How many times have you looked into the eyes of someone and discovered they had what we call "sleep" in their eyes? The first thing most of us do is cringe, right???? Yeah, I know…nasty looking, isn't it? What's even worse is to see sleep in the eyes of someone who wears a lot of dark mascara and eyeliner. I know…the first thing you say to yourself is uuugggggghhhhh! Right? It makes you want to take THEIR finger and show them where the goods are so they can get it out before it makes you sick. Am I right? Okay, I promise not to deal with the nose situation, because this could get a little ugly. What about the crust in the corner of the eye that settles there after you've washed your face a couple of times and dug out your eyeballs trying to ensure you've removed all the yuck-yuck that might embarrass you. How about thinking you wiped around your mouth after eating…but later on after reaching up to sweep the corners of your lips with your fingers, you discover that you missed some crumbs. How long had they been there…and why didn't someone tell you?

If you've encountered a similar situation with another person, would you get a Kleenex and make an attempt to help the person out or would you simply tell them that they have sleep in their eye, or crumbs around their mouth and they need to do something about it? In the natural, both of those scenarios would appear to be a good way to handle the situation, but in the spiritual and according to the above scripture, neither of them would be the first thing we should do. Why not…you might ask? Can I answer that question with a question? Have you looked in the mirror lately? Do you have that uuuggghhh thing going on in your eyes or crumbs around your mouth? In the above scripture, Jesus is teaching us to not criticize each other. I realize these examples may be a little gross to think about, but if we were doing anything that displeased God, think about how He would look upon us. We're talking about the mote in our brother's eye…but what about the larger one in ours?

It is so easy for us to think we have it all together. The Word of God can go forth, and it never applies to us…it simply goes right over our head. But we can always think of that next person who needed to hear that Word…that "mote" in our brother or sister's eye. I was in a situation where the Word of God went forth but I didn't feel like it was a Word for my present situation…so I didn't take it to heart. But oooh, I could think of someone who had done something to hurt me and thought…now so and so needed to be here to hear that Word…I hope somebody tells them about it. I was so quick to look at my brother or sister's mote and forgot about mine own. Believe me… we do it all the time. What about the devotions you receive daily? What about the ones you received this week? Did any of them apply to you or did they just happen to apply to someone else you knew? Did you forward it to them in hopes that God would step on their toes or that He would show them the error of their ways? Did you?! My point exactly! I believe that when the Word of God comes forth, it's intended for the one who heard or read it. You may not need it now, but you can be certain that you're going to need it later, so it's best to hold on to it. I know what I'm talking about because it's happened to me a number of times. There have been times when I thought the Word was for someone else, but then found myself dead smack in the middle of that very situation the Word for that day was speaking on. Have you ever been there? The Word of God does not go out and return unto Him void but it will accomplish what God sent it out to do (Isaiah 55:11 KJV); and that is to hit us and provoke us to change. The Word always has a purpose and a goal. If we hear it…we should receive it for ourselves FIRST. Do you remember the words of this song: 'Sweep around your own front door…before you try to sweep around mine?' That is a good example of what Jesus is saying in the above scripture. We have to make sure that our grass is cut before we talk about the neighbor's yard next door. We have to make sure that we don't have skeletons in our closet before we criticize someone's testimony of deliverance.

I've come to realize that nobody has a heaven or hell to put me in BUT God, and He is all that I am concerned with when it comes to being FREE!! We better learn to take our mouths off of other people before we find ourselves in situations we can't get out of. God is not pleased with that at all. Take a good long look in the mirror and ask God to show you areas in your life that you need to clean up... it could be PRIDE; it could be ENVY, it could be LUST; it could be HATRED; you might have a "know it all" spirit or have an "I'm all that and a bag of chips, Cool Ranch at that!" mentality. It could be a plethora of things hidden away in us that's not pleasing to God, but I guarantee you that when you sincerely ask Him to reveal them to you, He will magnify them for you. No one has it all together...we all have something that God needs to fix in us and our lives, but He can't fix those things if we can't see anything to be fixed. When I look in the mirror, I want my image to reflect HIS image...I want to see more of HIM and less of me. I want to be like David when he asked the Lord to create in him a clean heart and renew a right spirit within him. If my heart is clean, I won't be critical of others; if I have a renewed spirit, I can be diligent about seeking more of God. We all look in the mirror daily...as a matter of fact, you probably have a mirror sitting on your desk at work that you peek into from time to time throughout the day...checking your appearance...making sure there are no 'motes' or small particles in your eyes, your nose, or around your mouth. So while we are checking ourselves out...we should take time to ask God to reveal the beam in our eye, so that we are not so quick to see the mote in our brother or sister's eye.

I'm willing to bet that when you read the first paragraph of this Word today, the first thing you did was "checked yourself"...am I right? Did you grab a mirror and look to make sure you didn't have morning glory in your eyes? If you didn't have a mirror, did you reach up with your finger and check the corners of your eyes or wipe the corners of your mouth? If you did any of the above, then this Word has served its purpose. Always remember to check self FIRST before trying to 'CHECK' someone else. Be Blessed!

<u>Redeeming the Time</u>

See then that you walk circumspectly, not as fools, but as wise, redeeming the time, because the days are evil. Wherefore be ye not unwise, but understanding what the will of the Lord is. – Ephesians 5:15-17 KJV

As I was standing in my secret closet, I looked up and the Holy Spirit fell down upon me and filled my mouth! I thought, God…what am I praying about? What did you just have me pray for? Then I heard these words "redeeming the time." Do you remember the good old days when you were a child…the days when you didn't have a care in the world and absolutely no concept of time? In your mind, all there was for you to do was play. I mean, what else did you know to do when you were a child? Think about the times when you had a disagreement with your playmate or friend. To hurt you, they would talk about your mother…well, not really talk about her, but say something like, "Yo Mama." Out of retaliation and anger, you probably responded back with naaaw…Yo Mama! Then the two of you went back and forth with yo mamas until the fist fight broke out. After someone separated the two of you, they would ask "Why were you fighting?" The two of you would reply, because he/she was talking about my mama and nobody talks about my mama and gets away with it. A few hours later, you and your playmate or friend would make-up because there was still plenty of time left in the day to play, and you needed someone to play with. Without knowing it, as children, we knew how to redeem the time.

Now that you are an adult, does it seem to you that there just isn't enough time in the day for you to do all of the things you want or need to do? Twenty-four hours no longer feels like 24 hours but more like 12. What are you doing to redeem the time that you do have? In the above passage, Jesus was passing through the city and He took the opportunity to perform a miracle of healing. The disciples asked Jesus who sinned, this man or his parents? Jesus responded back to them, "neither hath this man sinned, nor his parents; but that the works of God should be made manifest in him." (John 9:3 KJV) Back then, Jewish culture believed that if you were afflicted, it was because you or someone in your family sinned, so it was common for that question to be asked. His disciples...the ones who walked with Him every day asked this question. They didn't get it, but Jesus was trying to show them what to do. He was redeeming the time He had while here on earth. We spend time griping and complaining about things that we can't change...like other people, when we should be redeeming the time or using it more wisely.

In the opening paragraph, I used children for an example because they really have no concept of time. They know better than we do how to take advantage of their playtime, because when night comes, they know they have to go to bed soon. On Saturdays they don't have to go to school, so most children are out of bed super early, so that they can get outside and play. First Corinthians 13:11 KJV reads, "When I was a child, I spoke as a child, I understood as a child, I thought as a child, but when I became a man (when I grew up...became an adult), I put away childish things." Just as the children were fighting in the example above...they made up and did it quickly. Do you mean to tell me that the children got this thing... but we as adults don't? We are still angry over something someone did to us a year ago...a month ago...how about yesterday or even in the past 12 hours?

I do not know about your schedules or what all has to be done in your day, but I do know this about mine; there is not enough time. I have God, my family, my job and my church. So what do we do when there isn't enough time in the day for it all? Well, we do what Jesus did...we redeem the time we have, and while we are in the world, we become "light" to the world. Light is used to help people "see." It is radiance, brightness, or illumination. It illuminates ones path to help them find where they are going. The opposite of it is darkness, night, gloom, or dusk. Night is a sign of distress as in Isaiah. 21...it represents death in John 9...ignorance in Mark 3 and evil in I Thessalonians 5. Jesus began His ministry at the age of 30 and laid down His life at the age of 33. Even at His birth, a light (star) shined bright in the night...indicating where He could be found. So even when He had no clue as a child what He would be...others already knew that He was the light. In those 3 years of His walk in ministry...He redeemed the time He had with vigor.

The Lord has you in the place you're in this very moment. Are you going to continue to waste the time you have or are you going to make good use of the time you have in that place? If there is someone you need to forgive, forgive them and move on. If you are living in darkness (sin) right now, repent and make a commitment to get it right from here until Jesus comes back. If you did someone wrong, go to them and apologize. Shine God's light in that dark situation. If you had an argument with a friend or family member, redeem the time and call them now and get it straightened out; even if you have to be the one who was wrong. Don't worry...God knows and He is taking care of the situation. I encourage you to redeem the time you are given each day. God gives us brand new mercies each and every day he allows us to open our eyes. Don't waste another moment arguing over petty things...Redeem the time! Don't waste another moment living in sin...Redeem the time! Don't waste another moment dreaming about your ministry...Redeem the time!! If the place God has you in is a dark place...He put you there because he needed His light there...so redeem the time while you have time. Be Blessed!

He is Waiting

Seek the Lord while you can find Him. Call on Him now while He is near. - Isaiah 55:6, NLT

Have you been going through something lately? How about THIS week? I mean really going through something...so much so that you didn't understand how you were going to deal with it. You've been tossing and turning...not sleeping at night.... frustrated with that thing and struggling with making decisions that you know will affect your life forever. Have you prayed and it just seems like God isn't hearing you? Are you crying out to Him in your frustration and He just seems so far away? Well I'm writing to tell you that God is yet near and He is waiting. Jesus says in Luke 11:9 KJV, "And I say unto you; Ask, and it shall be given you; seek and you shall find; knock, and it shall be opened unto you."

One sweet morning as I woke, I fell on my knees and began to pray... first giving thanks and then adoring my Savior; but as I got up from my knees, I began to hear one of the old songs we used to sing a long, long, long time ago. I will share it with you right now...because I believe in my heart that God wants to do something for someone reading this devotion TODAY...I believe that He is waiting this very moment to rescue someone TODAY! I believe that if you can just hear and conceive with a spiritual ear...you will get the answer you've been waiting on. I don't know about you, but I've been crying out to God and just hearing this song was a release for me that He is right here...and right now He wants me to confess my hurts, fears and my pains, so that He can come and see about little ole' me. See if you can remember this song...then let the melodies ring in your spirit...as a matter of fact, go ahead and sing it if you remember it...

> "Jesus is on the main line, tell Him what you want; Jesus is on the main line, tell Him what you want; Jesus is on the main line, tell Him what you want...you just call Him up

and tell Him what you want. If you're sick and you can't get well, tell him what you want; if you're sick and you can't get well, tell him what you want; if you're sick and you can't get well, tell him what you want...you just call Him up and tell Him what you want." Now right here, sing another verse by sticking in your issue and just tell Him what you want.

I was just thinking this morning how awesome God is and how He not only speaks into the atmosphere where all of his soldiers everywhere can hear Him, but He also speaks to His individual chosen ones. I don't know about you, but it does amazing things to my faith when God speaks directly to me and tells me, "daughter, this is what I want from you today...this is where I want you to go today...this is what I want you to say today! All I can say is Glory to God, Hallelujah, Thank You Jesus!!! Isn't it an awesome thing to know that He is leading and guiding your steps on a daily basis? The only way to get this is to seek Him early while He may be found.

Jesus is speaking in Luke 11:9 KJV, but He even says in verse 10 that those of us who ask, receives; those of us who seeks, finds; and those of us who knocks...it shall be opened unto us. What do you need from Him today? I can't fill your mouth today with the things you need of Him...only you know what it is you need from God...so ask Him. Don't be afraid and don't doubt. I believe without a doubt that He was speaking to me through that song and He wanted me to know that He was right there waiting on me...He is right here with me and He wants me to confess my needs to Him. If you're not in right relationship with Him, then you know you need to repent first and foremost. Forgiveness and salvation may be your need for today. If it is, I guarantee you that if you would just confess your faults to him, He is faithful and just to forgive you of your sins and not only that…but He will cleanse you of all unrighteousness. (1 John 1:9) So go ahead and confess that to Him today. If you need healing in your body, confess His word back to Him...by His stripes I am healed...but then ask that His Will be done in your situation. I dare you to trust Him...you have nothing to lose and everything to gain. Call Him up and tell Him what you want.

I want to pray with you today. Lord, God...we come before you... needing you like never before. In our frustrations God, we may have spoken some things that are not pleasing to you...so for those things we ask for your forgiveness. God, in our sufferings...in our pains... in our place of desolation, we sometimes don't know how to handle it...but we haven't quite realized God that you've never left us Lord... you've said it in your Word that you will never leave us nor forsake us, but we haven't quite gotten that in our hearts. THANK YOU GOD for letting us know that you are right here and that you are just waiting on us to seek you today...to seek you now because you want to deliver us from our suffering. You want to deliver us from our pain. You want to deliver us in our circumstances and situations. God we ask that you let your voice ring in our ears...let us hear what you want us to hear...and in our hearing...let it take root in our hearts. We know that there is a possibility that it may be a different answer than what we are expecting, but help us to know that YOU know what is best for us. We can't see everything that is ahead...but you can and some things in our lives are just distractions, keeping us from getting to the destination you have in mind for us. Thank you God for peace in our minds...peace in our spirits and peace in our hearts. In Jesus' name we pray, AMEN!

Sitting at His Right Hand

The LORD says to my lord, "Sit at my right hand until I make your enemies a footstool for your feet." - Psalms 110:1, NIV

There is a whole lot of power in the word of God! However, the power is of no use to us unless we know how to use it and apply it to our lives. This particular passage right here hit me in the gut one day, as I was talking to a co-worker of mine. As she was talking to me, the Holy Spirit dropped it on me to give to her. Now although I've heard it many, many times...it hit me really hard when it was given to me to share.

She had shared with me some time ago how she was treated by her peers and co-workers at one of her former jobs. They talked down to her, they scrutinized her work, they even gave her job to someone else...but they laid her off first in order to justify themselves. Through it all, she never fought back...she never opened her mouth to defend herself...she never retaliated! Right there, I could see that she was setting herself up for a blessing. As she was telling me those things, I told her not to worry about all of that...they are going to need you one day to do something for them. And sure enough, she copied me on an email that was sent to her from them. They needed her to stand in the gap for them...to help them get through the door of her current employer so that they could get some grant money. Look at God!! Look at how God humbled them to the point that they had to come back and ask her to help them...after they mistreated her. If we can just get to the place of knowing how powerful His word is! If we can just realize that we don't have to push...prime...or manipulate our circumstances; God has it all in control.

The scripture said, "Sit at my right hand", God's right hand...the straight and narrow...do what is "right" before Him and...BE STILL.... But then it says, "until". That means...don't move...don't squirm...be patient...WAIT...because when He shows up...He is going to show out!! But then the scripture tells us that He is going to make our enemy a footstool for our feet! This place where she worked was just a stepping stone for her to get to the place where God ultimately wanted to use her. Now He is using her to show them that you have to be careful how you treat others...because you never know when or if you will need them later in life. One of the things that God has put in me is to never burn bridges, because once they are burned you can't re-cross them...you can't go back over them. One day, you will see the people you left on the other side of that bridge you burned, and they will remember what you did while you were on that bridge.

We can't use the word of God on our enemies unless we are in the right place...a place of obedience...living a life pleasing to God! If you are dealing with the enemy right now...STOP IT!! Don't fight with him...don't buffet him or them...be still and know that God has it all under control. Do the right thing...be quiet, go to work, do your job... give more than the usual...then sit back and let God step in on your behalf. He will make your enemies your footstool.

Hide Him In Your Heart

Wherewithal shall a young man cleanse his way? by taking heed therefore, according to thy word. With my whole heart have I sought thee: O let me not wander from thy commandments. Thy word have I hid in mine heart, that I might not sin against thee. - Psalms 119:9-11 KJV

I use to wonder sometimes why people say some of the things that they say and do ALOT of the things that they do. But then the Holy Spirit brought back to my remembrance that I was once in the place of saying and doing. Although I wasn't an avid cursor or bad mouth person...if you made me really mad, my daddy would rise up out of me!!! Not my Godly Father...but my earthly father. There was one thing you didn't want to do...and that was make me mad!! I didn't have the power to hold my tongue or close my mouth like I do now... and ooh my goodness...I am so glad that God has done some major work on me. I use to do some things too...but I won't get into all of it at this time. Back then, I wasn't a reader of God's Word. I went to church, but I didn't read the Bible. I heard the Word preached over the pulpit, and yes, I did learn some things that way...but when I came into my own knowledge of God and His Word, it greatly changed my life and lifestyle.

The psalmist above not only asks us a question, but they give us the answer to that question. The scripture tells us how to cleanse ourselves and our ways. The way to do that is to take heed of what the Word of God tells us to do. It is not enough to memorize the scriptures...putting them to memory is good, but not enough. The scripture then tells us to use our whole heart to seek God and later to hide His commandments in our hearts. Well, why should we do that? We do it so that we might not sin against him. I can commit the word to memory and never know when to use it in my situation. The key is to hear the word and to walk in obedience to that word. First, when we hear or read the word, we should then process that word by committing it to our hearts, then we should put that word into action by using it when the opportunity arises. How will you know when to use it? You have to be sensitive to the Holy Spirit, because if the Word is hidden in your heart...the Holy Spirit will bring it back to you. It will ring out as clear as a bell...in the midst of that situation. I've had situations where I wanted to let someone have a piece of my mind...but right in the midst of them making me upset... the Holy Spirit would speak to me and say "Vengeance is mine and I will repay it." The Holy Spirit didn't tell me what book the scripture was found in...He didn't tell me what chapter...and neither did He tell me the verse number...all He had to tell me was "PEACE"...and my job was to smile at that person and say, "God Bless You."

Sometimes, we as Christians can be super-spiritual when it's not necessary. God just wants us to be doers of the Word. When we become doers and not hearers only, then we become examples to all of man-kind. Haven't we seen enough people talk a good word, but not living worth nothing? I know I have. And even though I see so much mess...in the church and out...I can't allow it to make me falter. Those people become stumbling blocks unto the ones who see them, and that is not pleasing to God. I admonish you to become a doer of the Word by hiding it in your heart so that you can use it when that time comes to use it. Hide it in your heart so that when the enemy tempts you, the Holy Spirit will lead and guide you to turn away from it...to resist it!

Hide the Word in your heart and watch how amazing things will change in your life. You will have strength in places you never thought you had...you will have confidence in knowing that God is right there with you...because...He is hidden in your heart...He is His Word! God Bless!

The Struggle is Over

But he that received seed into the good ground is he that heareth the word, and understandeth it; which also beareth fruit, and bringeth forth, some an hundred-fold, some sixty, some thirty. - Matthew 13:23 KJV

These words have been ringing in my spirit for quite some time and there is someone today that needs to hear and receive the following words I'm about to say, "The Struggle is over." Young man...young woman, did you hear what I said? Did you understand what I said? Are you ready to let the word manifest itself in your life? "The Struggle is Over"!!!

How long have you been in the same place, dealing with the same old issue...day in and day out? That man or woman who just won't leave you alone...who keeps on pulling at you or continues to call you when you've told them to leave you alone after you've made up your mind that you want to live a holy life!!!! Is the bill collector constantly calling and blowing up your phone, after you've told them you just didn't have the payment, but as soon as you get the money in your hand, you will send it to them? What about those holes in your pocket that keep swallowing up your finances to the point that you don't know how you are going to make it. Are you the one who's been sitting back watching as others were promoted and being blessed before you? Someone has waited and waited and waited on their ship to come in...but the ship has docked in someone else's port. I want to ask you these questions, have you been keeping the faith in your situation? Have you been applying the word of truth to your life and your situation?

I'm compelled to just share the words of this song right now, and if you have an ear to hear, then receive it in Jesus name. "The struggle is over. The struggle is over. The struggle is over for you. You've been in this place long enough and your mountain side has been rough, the struggle is over for you! The heartache is over. The heartache is over. The heartache is over for you. You've been in this place long enough and your mountain side has been rough, the struggle is over for you."

Whatever you've been struggling with; finances, sexual sin… fornication, adultery, masturbation, lust, a dirty mouth, pride, hatred, strife, gossip, backbiting…whatever it might be…grab hold of the truth that is coming your way. Have itchy ears to hear what the spirit is saying in your situation because I'm telling you now…I feel in my spirit that God's about to release an anointing of deliverance to those who are READY. Are you ready for your struggle to end? Are you really ready for your struggle to end? The word is going to come and those who have an ear to hear, those who need to be released from a stronghold in their life, those willing to apply the word to their situation, those ready to bear fruit are going to be the ones who will reap the one hundred fold, the sixty fold, and the thirty fold blessings.

I don't know about you, but I'm ready for the one hundred fold blessing…but if God sees fit to give me the thirty…I'm not going to hate on the one who got the one hundred fold. I want us all to be blessed in Jesus name! Get your ground ready! It's time to walk in a new season of harvest…a new season is ahead of you and if you can just believe God's word today…if you can just receive it in your spirit man…God is ready to do something in your life. Be ready… because "Your Struggle is Over!!!" Hear it and receive it in Jesus' mighty name!!

Don't Let Ignorance Be Your Excuse

Ye shall have one law for him that sinneth through ignorance, both for him that is born among the children of Israel, and for the stranger that sojourneth among them. But the soul that doeth ought presumptuously, whether he be born in the land, or a stranger, the same reproacheth the Lord; and that soul shall be cut off from among his people, because he hath despised the word of the Lord, and hath broken his commandment, that soul shall utterly be cut off; his iniquity shall be upon him. - Numbers 15:29-31 KJV

I'm struggling with how to deal with this subject, because ignorance is such a very strong word, and people use it as a tool to manipulate. But do you know that God knows our heart and every one of our thoughts? We can only play stupid for so long and then we have to be held accountable for our actions. Ignorance simply means without knowledge or comprehension, **stupidity**; unaware, or the inability to give attention. We can let children get away with some of the things they do simply because they may not know any better and are still in the process of learning. We can excuse people with mental disabilities because we know they can't comprehend right from wrong.

Given the fact that we have been graced with a new year and some unfulfilled promises are waiting to be released, we have to have our minds made up that the stupid stuff we allowed to hold us back in years prior will not prosper going forward. Don't be fooled...the enemy hasn't forgotten about you and neither has he forgotten about your areas of weakness or struggle. Although he didn't kill you, he succeeded in stealing some things from you...your joy...your hope... your finances...your focus, your family members...your purpose, or maybe even some dreams. For some of you, he was successful in stealing your testimony by causing you to do some stupid stuff like giving into sin...whether fornication, gossip, adultery, swearing, backbiting, gambling (whether going to the casino or getting someone to buy you a lotto ticket), lying, or even stealing. But in this new season, God would not have us to be ignorant concerning the enemy's devices. He has not given us the spirit of fear, but of power, love, and a sound mind! Because we have a sound mind, we must be aware of the tactics the enemy used against us in the past and recognize them when they are coming up against us again; so the next time we encounter those situations, we can defeat the enemy in them. We should not be guilty of the same stuff because now we are no longer stupid...ignorant...unaware; we are wiser through experience.

Before the clock struck midnight last night, the enemy had already strategized his plan of attack on you. He looked back over your past, and at all the tactics he had used that caused you to doubt God, to falter in your faith, to become discouraged, to lose hope, to abandon your purpose, to stagnate or idle your mind, or to slow down your process for deliverance. He then put those things back on his "to-do list", with your name attached to it, as he waits...lurking to and fro...for the perfect opportunity to make his sneak attack. He hits you when and where you are most vulnerable. The key to defeating him is to remember where that vulnerability is and be prepared for it when the enemy comes in like a flood. If you recognize now where that area is...it's time to go on a fast...to crucify that flesh and ask God to help you strengthen that area. Remember, even Jesus went on a fast for 40 days and 40 nights because He would be tempted of the devil. He was tired, alone, and hungry, and therefore vulnerable in those areas where Satan tried to tempt Him. But Jesus didn't give in and neither should we.

In the Old Testament, God set the law in place that anyone who unknowingly sinned could be forgiven when they brought the specific stated sin offering, but in the New Testament, God uses repentance to free one from sin. It is so easy to use repentance as an excuse to sin, but the scripture says that those who sin intentionally, their soul shall be cut off. But what happens when the opportunity to repent is not allowed? Think about it? Would you want to risk going to hell for that little mistake you are about to make? Would you risk turning your soul over to burn in the lake of fire forever and ever? Can you deal with standing by watching while others get blessed... knowing that you got out of line because of stupidity? Don't allow the enemy to keep you blinded by letting ignorance be your excuse. Be Blessed!

Invite Him in Your Prayer Closet

But ye, beloved, building up yourselves on your most holy faith, praying in the Holy Ghost. Keep yourselves in the love of God, looking for the mercy of our Lord Jesus Christ unto eternal life. - Jude 20-21, KJV

Do you have days when you fall on your knees to pray, but you just can't find the words to say? Maybe it's not that you can't find the words, but maybe you don't want to be monotonous in your prayer to the Lord. You want to make sure that you are not saying the same old thing every time you bend your knees. I have found myself in that place on many occasions. The first thing I do when I get down to pray is praise and adore God for who He is...He is good, He is merciful...He is kind...He is magnificent and precious to me because He loved me enough to send His Son to die for me. Then I offer up thanks for just waking me up another morning... letting me see another day...for protecting me through dangers seen and unseen...shielding me from accidents...keeping my family safe and healthy...giving me a good job...a roof over my head...food on the table and clothes on our backs. Then I get to the place where I'm searching for words...I don't know what to pray for next...I'm not sensing a particular person or thing in my spirit that I need to pray for or about...yet I know that I should be interceding for someone else because I know that God knows I'm grateful for all of the things He has given me and done for me...I make it a point to tell Him every day.

So this is where I shut up...I pause for a moment of silence...I sit still and allow the Holy Spirit to come in and take over. Because I know that even my little, finite mind doesn't compare to the mind of Christ... and if I allow the Sprit to take over my prayer...He's going to make sure that those things I really need to pray about will get prayed for. It is here, in my quietness…in my state of complete stillness... that the Holy Spirit begins to reveal to me who and what I need to pray for. He begins dropping people into my Spirit...situations that I haven't considered...people close to me who may be hiding within their hurt and don't have the courage to ask someone else to pray for them. But if I get up too quickly, once I've prayed for myself, then I may miss the opportunity to intercede on someone else's behalf. I may miss what the Holy Spirit is trying to reveal to me; all because I got up too quickly...all because I was in a rush to get back to the mundane things of life...all because I didn't have time to listen to God. Communication is a two way process...sending and receiving. If only one person is talking...then there is no communication...you're just talking. In prayer, you send up your requests and God sends down His response. God doesn't want you to be the only one talking. He has something to say too. But all too often we're focused on what God can do for us, not what we can do for God. And many times, all He wants is for someone to stand in the gap for others...and it won't cost us anything but time.

There are people around you today that stand in the need of something from God...it could be emotional healing...it could be physical healing...it could be that a loved one needs protection or to be saved...it could be a financial breakthrough...in whatever case... when you go into your prayer closet...after there are no more words to say...just sit quiet for a moment. You may be surprised what things God reveals to you in that quiet time. And before you know it, your five minute prayer has turned into 15 minutes, then 30...then 45, until you've completely lost track of time. Once we learn to allow the Holy Spirit to have His way in our prayer time, you will have prayed for people that you had no clue to pray for and God will be glorified. Don't get me wrong, it's not about the length of your prayer. God is not sitting up in heaven with a time clock, recording the number of minutes that we spend in prayer. God is looking at our hearts and its sincerity.

In closing, I believe God wants to say something to you in your prayer time today. Do you have time to listen? If you do, then don't hesitate to invite Him into your prayer closet. Be Blessed!

Don't Try to Understand It, Just Trust HIM!

Scripture: Trust in the LORD with all thine heart; and lean not unto thine own understanding. In all thy ways acknowledge Him and He shall direct thy paths. Proverbs 3:5 & 6, KJV

People of God today! I realize we are in the midst of a very shaky season for any and everyone walking upon the face of the earth. If we were to look at what's happening right now with our natural eyes...we would call this a day of doom and gloom. When we hear what's going on with our natural ears...we might hear devastation and desolation...people all over the world being let go on their jobs...forced to retire sooner than expected...folks being laid off... companies closing their doors temporarily and permanently. But People of God...we must hear what God is saying to us as a people. This is not the time for despondency...this is a time for us to turn our faces to the wall...this is the time to continue trusting God...this is the time for us to see and hear what's going on in the Spirit realm! If you are a believer today...I urge you to turn away from what you see and hear in the natural and put your faith and trust in God. We must put our focus on what's happening in the spiritual atmosphere. Has God done anything for you up to now?

Do I have to remind you that He is the same yesterday, today, and forever? God has not changed people! Do you hear me?!! Might I remind you that God is the same God who provided food, water, clothing, and a multitude of riches for the 4 Lepers sitting outside the gates of Samaria; He's the same God that caused Joseph to go through major storms in his life...only to set him up to feed his family during a time of famine; He's the same God that fed the multitude...I mean literally thousands with only 5 loaves of bread and 2 fish! So whether you understand the times right now or not... You have got to trust God in the midst of these times.

Proverbs 7 & 8 reads, "Be not wise in thine own eyes; fear the LORD, and depart from evil. It shall be health to thy navel, and marrow to thy bones." The navel is a very insignificant part of your body now that you are out of your mother's womb. But when you were in her womb, the umbilicus or umbilical cord (navel) was of the utmost significance. Why? The umbilical cord carried "death or life" from your mother to you while you were in your prenatal stages of life. Again, it is the flexible tube that carries oxygen and nutrients to the growing fetus from the mother, and also carries waste products away from the baby so that the mother's body might eliminate them. For a moment, what if the umbilicus malfunctioned...what if the waste never traveled from your system through that tube to your mother's system....what if it crossed along the way? God created this thing and He knows the outcome...or just how it works; just like He knows the outcome of your situation. I don't know what you are going through...but the ALL-Knowing...ALL-Seeing God does. If the umbilical cord was the "life-line" while you were in your mother's womb, you must know that God is your "life-line" now that you are out.

I believe He sent these words because He knows that right now, someone is going through a situation that is about to make them lose their mind. Someone is dealing with some circumstances that they haven't told anyone about...because if they did, all "you know what" would break loose. Someone is hiding behind their pain and just needs to know that GOD is aware of their situation. God wants you to know that He is God and no situation that you are going through is too hard for Him to solve. He is the great 'I AM." He is the first and the last, the beginning and the end. He can handle any situation or circumstance that has you bound. If you would just recognize that He is Jehovah-Shammah – The Lord is there; He never leaves. He is Jehovah-Jireh; your provider. He is Jehovah-Shalom; He is your Peace...whatever you need...He is!!!

Get this...you don't have to jeopardize your integrity for anyone or anything. Be still and know that He is God...He is Jehovah-Nissi; The Lord your Banner, and any battle that you are in...give it to the Lord for it is not yours, but it is His. He just wants you to hold on...

don't give up…wait on Him…Trust HIM…He is God! Even when you don't understand why you've been dealing with this thing for so long…Trust HIM. But they that wait upon the LORD shall renew their strength; they shall mount up with wings as eagles; they shall run, and not be weary; and they shall walk, and not faint. Don't try to understand it…just trust Him!!! God Bless.

If You Are Being Obedient, A Rewards Awaits You

This book of the Law shall not depart out of they mouth; but thou shalt meditate therein day and night, that thou mayest observe to do according to all that is written therein; for then thou shalt make thy way prosperous, and then thou shalt have good success. Have not I commanded thee? Be strong and of a good courage; be not afraid, neither be thou dismayed; for the Lord they God is with thee withersoever thou goest." – Joshua 1:8-9 KJV

Obedience is a hard subject to deal with especially when it comes to people. Why? Because we have developed the mindset that as long as we are grown, we can do what we want to do; go where we want to go; say what we want to say; live how we want to live...you get where I am going??? There are times when we disregard man made laws...speeding, running stop signs, illegal parking, etc. But with all of that...there are yet consequences. I'm sure you have some past experiences that you can share in which you weren't obedient and had to pay the consequences for having a hard head...right? Even as a child, I can remember having a sore bottom for having a hard head. The rod was in no way spared in my parent's household. If we were told to do something, we had better find ourselves doing it immediately after the instruction was given. I can remember being told to wash dishes; but my favorite television show was just about to go off. I'm talking maybe 3 minutes left...of Good Times. It was just 3 minutes left and I stayed put in front of the tube until the credits started to roll...but nooo, my mother wouldn't wait on me! Because I didn't move upon her command...within 60 seconds, I was feeling a sharp pain going across my rear end, from one of my dad's large leather belts. Her words were, "Didn't I ('whap') tell you ('whap') to go ('whap') and wash ('whap') them dishes ('whap whap whap?") 😣 My response was always, I was on my way to wash them...you didn't give me enough time. Her reply back would be, "you were supposed to move when I told you to move, not when you get ready to move." Ahaaaah, and there we have the problem. She is my mother...as long as I was instructed to do something, there should not have been any questions nor hesitation, just obedience. Nevertheless, I am going through the same thing with my children, 40 years later than when I was taking here through the ringer with my disobedience.

For a few days, God kept sending me back to read the first chapter of Joshua because He wanted me to reveal some things, not just to me, but to someone else that will read this today. In this Day... Moses dies and Joshua is commissioned by the Lord to take the children of Israel into the Promised Land. The children of Israel had just come out of their 40 year "wilderness" experience because of disobedience, and now were getting ready to walk over into the Land of Promise. But before they could cross over...they were given some instructions they had to follow. First, they had to study the Word of God...meditate on it day and night. Then they had to follow the instructions given according to the word...God's Book of Law... the Bible. He said to observe to do according to all that is written in it. After we do this, what can we expect? If we do just what God's words tells us to do, don't cheat, don't lie, don't steal, don't backbite, don't fornicate, don't commit adultery, don't covet, love one another, pray for one another....and the list goes on...then shall our way be made prosperous...successful...flourishing...thriving...well off. But then the Lord reinforces His word by telling us to be strong (sturdy, well-built, tough); and have good courage (brave, gutsy, daring); stand up to the enemy because He is with us.

When I thought about this, I realized that I have missed out on so many blessings that I could be enjoying right now because of my disobedience. If you examined yourself today, would you be able to say that you are being obedient to the Word of God in every area of your life? I can say this, that I have fallen short for many years, but I thank God for His new mercies every day, because that means that what didn't get worked on yesterday, can be worked on today. I believe that we all are considered by God as "a work in progress," which means that with each new day given, we can get better and better. Each day I'm striving to bring my entire life...my work life, my home life, and my church or spiritual life into obedience of God's Word. And I admonish you today to examine your life. If you are walking in obedience in every area...a reward awaits you; but if you aren't, continue to work at it and let God know that you are at least trying. When we finally get it right like the children of Israel did, we will be able to obtain not just heavenly rewards when we die... but He will give us some of the earthly rewards He has waiting on us. Be Blessed

Are You Ready to Be Complete?

Being confident of this very thing, that He which hath begun a good work in you will perform it until the day of Jesus Christ. – Philippians 1:6, KJV

This scripture right here brings me so much comfort. I find comfort in knowing that God is not finished with me and He won't be finished with me until Jesus returns to take me home with Him. When I think about all that I haven't done yet, and all that I desire to do for the Kingdom of God, I don't believe that He is finished with me just yet. Here we are looking at another year... I know tomorrow is not promised to me, but at least I have today. But what if my time was up tomorrow? What if it's up next week? I found out that the #7 was a very powerful number and it is very symbolic to God. Why? Well, when I began to research the #7, I found out that it is the number of completion. Well, if it is the number of completion, what could my being allowed to see a new year mean for me? I believe it means that some things that God has set in motion for me up to this time will come to fruition in this next year. I made an attempt to look up the word 'perform' and what I found out about the word perform is, it means to do...to carry-out, to execute, to achieve...to complete! Did you hear what I said??? It means to complete!! I believe that God has prepared to catapult His soldiers to a place in Him that we've never seen before...a place that will amaze our little finite minds and blow our intellect all to pieces. The Bible says that every good and perfect gift comes from God...and our reference scripture tells us that the work that God began in us when we accepted His Son into our lives is GOOD! But the most awesome part of that scripture tells us that we can be CONFIDENT (sure...certain...positive...secure) that He will COMPLETE the work He began.

Now when I started out studying this word, this is not where it was going. I was supposed to write about the importance of the #7 to God. When I began researching that number in the Bible, I initially got started because of a dream. Although I'm not at liberty to share the dream, I can try to put in words where it took me. After waking up from this dream, I was sent to Revelations to read. I don't have to explain to you what the book of Revelations is all about, but if you don't know and want to know, you better take the time to read it for yourself. Just to give you a tidbit of the importance of the #7 to God, in the book of Revelations, Days 2 & 3, God talks about The Seven Churches: #1 The Church of Ephesus (**The Loveless Church**), #2 The Church of Smyrna (**The Persecuted Church**), #3 The Church of Pergamos (**The Lenient Church**), #4 The Church of Thyatira (**The Compromising Church**), #5 The Church of Sardis (**The Lifeless Church**), #6 The Church of Philadelphia (**The Obedient Church**) and #7 The Church of Laodiceans (**The Lukewarm Church**). After I finished reading about these, I began to get frightened. I didn't get frightened because of my church...because I can't judge where my church sits in that number, but I do know that as long as I'm a servant of God...as long as I'm dedicated to delivering God's Word... as long as I'm here on this earth, I better find myself under the church of Philadelphia...a church that is obedient to the word of God. I want to make sure that my life reflects obedience to God's Word. There are other important factors in the Bible that reference the #7 and are important to God, such as **The Seven Angels** who holds **The Seven Trumpets** and **The Seven Vials**. When those seven trumpets are blown, unbelievers will have an opportunity to repent, but when those seven vials are opened...it will be too late. The trumpets represent grace, but the vials represent God's wrath... His judgment. Once God's wrath is poured upon the face of the earth no man who hasn't repented will be able to repent.

After I read all of this, I just began to tremble at the thought of it all and what it could mean. So the first thing I did was begin to examine myself...because I'm the one who had the dream. Secondly, I began to repent for any hidden sins or things that I may have been blind to...because we sometimes do or say things that are not pleasing to God, not even realizing that we are sinning. Thirdly, I began to share this with people, such as I am doing today. God wants us to get this thing right because He wants to take us all with Him at His return.

It is not my desire to frighten anyone, but we are to live each day as if Jesus was returning today. In Proverbs 6:16-19 KJV, the Bible references seven things that God hates: (1) a proud look, (2) a lying tongue, (3) hands that shed innocent blood, (4) a heart that deviseth wicked imaginations, (5) feet that be swift in running to mischief, (6) a false witness that speaketh lies, and (7) he that soweth discord among brethren. When God spoke about each of the churches, He ended with "He that hath an ear, let him hear what the Spirit saith unto the church." There are times when people accept Christ, but haven't let go of the world. If you have found yourself in any of those places we just spoke of, then your time is now. If you are ready to be complete in God...then hear the word of the Lord today and receive your complete deliverance. Some of us will be complete in healing...some in deliverance...some in your ministry...some in your finances...some in personal relationships...some in marriages... some in singleness, so get ready man of God. Prepare yourself woman of God. Are you ready to be complete?!!!

Do You Know Him?

Today, I don't have a particular Scripture to concentrate on, but it has been impressed upon my heart to share with you in knowing God. The One we call our Father. The One we call upon when we're in trouble. The One who knows all about our insecurities and insufficiencies but loves us nevertheless. Do you know Him? Do you really know Him? If you know Him, then why are you fretting? If you know Him, then why don't you trust Him? If you know Him, then why are you trying to fix that problem with your own power? If you know Him, then, why don't you take your hands off of the situation and let Him handle it for you? Step back, let it go, and let God arise in your life.

Who is God? I'm glad you asked. James Cleveland penned the song, "God Is." See if you can remember these words to the chorus ringing in your spirit. "God is the Joy and the Strength of my life; He moves all pain, misery and strife. He promise to keep me, never to leave me. He's never ever come short of His Word. I've got to fast and pray, stay in His narrow way, I've got to keep my life clean everyday; I want to go with Him when He comes back, I've come to far and I'll never turn back." God is. God is my all in all."

While hearing this song, I went back and began to think about who God is. As I thought about Him, the song really began to bless me. In Genesis 22:13-14 KJV, Abraham realized that God was Jehovah-Jireh; (the Lord will provide) when God provided the ram in the bush as a sacrifice instead of using his own child as a sacrifice. Abraham trusted God because he knew Him. Not only is He a provider, but He is a Healer too! Do you remember the woman with the issue of Blood? She had the disease for twelve long years but she trusted that if she could just touch the hem of Jesus' garment, she would be healed. What about Naaman and his leprosy? God is Jehovah-Rapha; the Lord that healeth thee (Exodus 15:26 KJV).

Do you wonder whether God is aware of your situation? Of course He is because He is Omniscient. He is all knowing. Think about this. You are somewhere minding your own business when suddenly you read something or hear something, or someone has spoken into your life and you wonder if they were peeking through your window. Not only that, you wonder who could have told your business. What happens is God sends a Word to let you know that He is aware of your situation, and because He is aware, He wants you to be assured that He is right there, covering you as you go through your trials and tribulations. The truth of the matter is God knew exactly where you would be, what time you would be there, and what you would be doing at the time the Word came to you. God orchestrates stuff just like that. He sets us up when we're not even aware of it.

First John 3:20 KJV reads, "For if our heart condemn us, God is greater than our heart, and knoweth all things." There are times when my mind wanders or becomes judgmental and I have to bring those thoughts back, because I realize that God would not be pleased for me to be thinking those things. I don't wonder, I know He knows what I'm thinking. This helps to keep me in check. The song says that I have stay in His narrow way and keep my life clean everyday. If God is all-knowing then why are you worrying about your situation? God is mindful of you and He won't put more on you than you can bear. If you are going through the fire, be reminded of Job. He was tested of Satan by permission. But the key thing about Job is he was blameless. He was living the words of the above James Cleveland's song. He couldn't understand why he was going through but God allowed it because He knew he could handle it. If you are going through something right now, let me encourage you to hold on. He hasn't forsaken you. Although He may be on the other side of town tending to another soul, He is yet still with you because He is omnipresent; He is present everywhere at the same time.

I pray that it will bring you comfort to know that God is eternal; He is immutable or unchangeable. He is righteous. He is just. He is merciful. He is faithful and He is Holy. Don't let your situation or circumstances put God in a box because He can't be measured. Trust Him today.

I AM GOD!

Readers, one morning I had an overwhelming experience with the Lord on my ride in to work. I'm usually out of the house at 6:30 headed to work, but I was running a little later than usual, and I believe the Lord purposed for this to happen because He wanted to minister to someone who's going to read this. I believe that there is someone out there who needs to know who God is…and He is getting ready to tell you as the following song ministers to your spirit. Whatever it is you are going through…God wants you to grab hold to the words of this song, and if you can remember the tune, sing it until you feel it in your spirit. I know that I wanted to pull my car over onto the side of the road and run until the spirit let go of me…but I kept my composure! As people beside and in front of me watched on, trying to figure out why I was driving with my hand held to the sky, I continued to give God the praise because He was talking to me through song! Glory to God, Hallelujah!!! I will stop right now in the midst of this praise so you can get it too!! Be Blessed and know that He Is GOD!!

I am God all by myself, I don't need any help.
I can handle things on my own.
I am the first and the last, whatever you need just ask,
for I am, I am, I am God.

I was there in the beginning,
and I'll be there when you get to the end.
I am all seeing, all knowing, Almighty, ever showing;
for I am, I am, I am God.

By Songwriters: Donald Lawrence and The Tri-City Singers

(And you know how the rest of the song goes)

God wants you to see something even in this song. The penman of this song had to put repeated lyrics in-order for the song to be able to minister to us, "But I, The Lord, am repeating this to you because you don't really understand who I AM. You say you trust me, You say that you are my child, You say that you Love Me, but I'm not feeling that from you. Must I continue to prove to you that I AM JEHOVAH JIREH, I'm your Provider? Must I continue to tell you that I AM JEHOVAH NISSI, I'll fight your battles? I know everything that you are going through, did you forget that I'M ALL KNOWING? Just know that I AM GOD!"

Whomever this is for, don't let another minute go by without recognizing who GOD IS! Blessings!

It's Time to Pull Down Our Strongholds

For though we walk in the flesh, we do not war after the flesh: For the weapons of our warfare are not carnal, but mighty through God to the pulling down of strong holds; Casting down imaginations, and every high thing that exalteth itself against the knowledge of God, and bringing into captivity every thought to the obedience of Christ; And having in a readiness to revenge all disobedience, when your obedience is fulfilled. – II Corinthians 10:3-6 KJV

I feel very strongly that God is trying to reach someone who is reading this daily meditation today. The Lord spoke into my Spirit that it is time for us to pull down the strongholds in our lives. Wherefore (as the Holy Ghost saith), Today if ye will hear his voice, harden not your hearts. This day...the day you read this word...harden not your heart. He is commanding us to pull them down! Why? Because they are tools and tactics of the enemy; and He (God) that is in you is greater than he (Satan) that is in the world. Strongholds are things that keep you from completely serving God. Rev. 3:15-16 KJV reads: "I know thy works, that thou art neither cold nor hot: I would thou wert cold or hot. So then because thou art lukewarm, and neither cold nor hot, I will spue thee out of my mouth." If you say that you belong to God...prove it. That thing that has you bound... pull it down! That person who has you on that string working you like a yo-yo and a puppet...pull them down! That hindering habit you have...pull it down! That gossiping tongue...pull it down! That backbiting spirit...pull it down! You know more than I what you are dealing with and all you have to do is pull it down!

I feel like I need to minister to someone right now who can't seem to quit fornicating or indulging in ungodly flesh acts. How long must God wait on you to make up in your mind that you want to be delivered of that demon that has you bound? "You do know that this is not a carnal battle...but you have to use the power I've put inside of you to say NO to the enemy," says the Lord. "You do not have to answer those telephone calls and neither do you have to open that door when he or she comes by. I have given you the keys to life. Do you want to continue in sin that grace may abound? I forbid," says the Lord. "This day, harden not your heart. Listen for my voice... my sheep know my voice. Obey my Word! If you love me, keep my commandments. Obedience is the gateway to deliverance. How can you say you love me when you don't keep my commandments? I've commanded you to love your enemies. How can you love me if you aren't loving your enemies and praying for those who despitefully use you?"

I realized that this may not be going in the direction I intended this devotion to go today, but God said that His word shall accomplish what it was sent to do. I believe someone needs to hear that God is waiting on them to stop their mess. For some of you, your stronghold may not be fornication or a weakness in your flesh; perhaps it's backbiting, overspending, overeating (gluttony), lying, lust, stealing, pride, envy or jealousy, etc. Just like God is waiting on them to get it right; He's waiting on the rest of us to get it right too. Today, God says...PULL THEM DOWN; whatever it is. I believe that God does not want any lukewarm soldier...in and out of the battle...don't know whether we are coming or going. Not only are we a hindrance to ourselves; we are a stumbling block to others. We better learn that if God be for us, He is more than the whole world against us. That's why Romans 6:11 KJV says, "Likewise reckon ye also yourselves to be dead indeed unto sin, but alive unto God through Jesus Christ our Lord."

As I tried to increase this devotion to a longer version, God sent a sign that I was getting in the flesh, so I am cutting it off right here. I asked the Lord to use me any way He sees fit. So I yield to Him when I sense His Spirit, but when He leaves me...I must stop. With that said, I would not end this devotion without us praying for God's forgiveness and restoration. If you know that you are not serving God and only God this very moment, pray this prayer with me. Father, we come to you this moment with bowed down heads, uplifted hearts, and minds ready to serve you. God you know when we are in our weakest moments...and during those times God, you've always made a way of escape that we might be able to bear that temptation. But God, we didn't heed the warning signs...we ignored the power to resist the enemy, because we wanted to satisfy our nasty old flesh. Today, we ask your forgiveness for yielding to the enemy...for giving in and letting him have his way in and with us, in Jesus Name. We ask that you come into our hearts right now Father, in Jesus Name. Create in us a clean heart, and renew a right spirit within us. As we give our lives back over to you, we will vow to teach others your way oh God, that others might know you as we do. We thank you now for your grace and mercy that has allowed us to come this far; but we will no longer take it for granted. We love you, praise you, honor and adore you. All these things we pray in your precious Son, Jesus' name. Amen. Be Blessed!

What Do You Do When Resisting Doesn't Work?

Blessed is the man who endures temptation; for when he has been approved, he will receive the crown of life which the Lord has promised to those who love Him. – James 1:12, NKJV (background from Genesis 39)

Is there anybody reading this word right now who knows what it's like to be tried and tested on every side?! If you're not ashamed to admit that you've been tempted to do something outside of the Will of God...then you can be delivered. If the truth be told, somebody reading this word is facing some form of temptation this very moment. Ask me how I know? I'm glad you asked...Because the enemy is on his job. We would be foolish to think that Satan's tactics have changed...no ma'am and no sir; his tactics are still the same... he just uses the same old tricks on new people. Do you know why the enemy is so confident in his devices? He's confident because he knows his stuff. He knows exactly what has worked on each one of us in the past, and he knows that if he keeps trying us long enough... eventually we just might allow him to slip in.

Did you know that the enemy can't do anything except God allows him ? I believe it would be safe to say that every one of us has fallen for the same trick at least twice...am I right? Some of us may even be going through the same test today, simply because we still haven't gotten it right. But how many of you know that when you fail the test...you have to take it all over again? Amen... My Bible tells me about a certain man by the name of Joseph who's had his share of adversity. His story is a great depiction of "Courage under Fire," Why? Joseph's been tried and tested on every side, beginning with envy and jealousy from his own loved ones, to being thrown in a pit to die, then being pulled out of the pit only to be sold into slavery. This brings us to our Day of focus: Genesis 39. In this Day, we will find that Satan consistently tried Joseph in the same area - the area of temptation....day after day after day. If I could just elaborate on the story for just a moment; Joseph was a strikingly handsome young man. As it turned out, God was with Joseph and things went very well for him. He went from working in the field to managing the King's mansion. Joseph ended up living in the home of his Egyptian master by the name of Potipher. Potipher even recognized that God was with Joseph. He saw that God was working for good in everything Joseph did. As a result of the favor of God on Joseph's life, Potipher became very fond of Joseph and made him his personal aide. He put him in charge of all his personal affairs, turning everything over to him. From that moment on, God blessed the home of Potipher—all because of who? Joseph! But why did God do that? First, Joseph had 'integrity' which is something a whole bunch of us lack these days. Not only could God trust him, Potipher found that he could trust him as well. Because of Joseph's integrity, the blessings of God spread over everything Potipher owned, at home and in the fields, and all Potipher had to concern himself with was eating three meals a day. How many of you have someone in your life you can put your trust in like that? (I didn't think so) Back to the story! As time went on, Potipher's wife became infatuated with Joseph and one day, when she just couldn't stand it any longer (NOW LOOK OUT...HERE COMES THE TEMPTATION) she says to Joseph, "Sleep with me." But what does Joseph do?

The first thing he did was (1) He kept his focus. Joseph focused on his job and not on the object of his temptation, Potipher's wife, who was aggressively pursuing him. At the peak of her aggression, Joseph did something amazing: he stopped, took a high-level view of the situation, and clearly laid out why he would never fall for her enticement. Joseph thought on not only the natural ramifications of giving in to temptation, but he also weighed the spiritual consequences. Look at what he told Potipher's wife, "Look, with me here, my master doesn't give a second thought to anything that goes on here—he's put me in charge of everything he owns. He treats me as an equal. The only thing he hasn't turned over to me is you. After all, you're his wife! How then could I violate his trust (he's talking about Potipher 'the natural') and sin against God?" (the spiritual). Joseph feared God! It's time out for us to stop giving in to temptation and saying "the devil made me do it." The word of God says in James

1:12-14 NIV, "Blessed is the man who perseveres under trial, because when he has stood the test, he will receive the crown of life that God has promised to those who love him." When tempted, no one should say, "God is tempting me." For God cannot be tempted by evil, nor does he tempt anyone; but each one is tempted when, by his own evil desire, he is dragged away and enticed. (NIV)" Let me get back to the story. As Potipher's wife continued to pester Joseph day after day after day, he continued to stand his ground. He refused to go to bed with her. Now, don't get this thing mixed up. This is more than just a story of lust…you've got to see the integrity Joseph had during his test and the value he placed on his relationship with God.

One of the enemy's chief tactics is to keep our attention focused intently on the object of our desire…such as he did with Potipher's wife. If Satan can keep our eyes on what we long to possess, then he knows he already has us beat. Satan is the ruler of darkness and if he can keep us in the dark, then he can keep us from getting victory over our situations. Satan's job is 3 fold, he comes to steal, kill, and destroy! The enemy desires for us to walk around with blinders on every day…not knowing where to go or which way to turn. Do you know that it is important to have discernment? Joseph not only had wisdom…but he had discernment too! It is imperative that we not be ignorant of Satan's devices…he has no new tricks…he's just using the same old ones on different people and he's even using some of the same old tricks on some of the same old people because he knows that we haven't figured it out yet! If you failed the test once… guess what…you have to take it over again.

One day Joseph goes back to the house to do his work and none of the household servants happened to be there. Now right here… Joseph's discernment kicks in…because I'm sure he's already figured out that Potipher's wife has got to be somewhere around. If I could just use my sanctified imagination right about now…I can see Joseph standing in the room…as he turns around, there she is… she's standing between him and the door. Now she thinks she's got him cornered because he would have to walk by her in order to get out of the room. Now if could just imagine a little more, Joseph starts calling out to God, Ooooh God…you see God…and you know God…

God...it's not my desire to sin against you...I need you now God...I need you to deliver me...deliver me from the hands of the enemy...I know you can God and I know you will! Then right at the moment she reaches and grabs him by his cloak, saying, "Sleep with me!" Suddenly, God gives Joseph the way of escape. What does Joseph do? Joseph gains "Courage under fire" and he runs out of the house, leaving her standing there with his garment in her hand.

Now I presented the title to you today in question form, so if I were to go back and ask you again...when resisting isn't working, what do you do? Maybe you've been in a situation where you've been tempted to do evil instead of good. If you're like Paul, he said when he would do good...evil is present with him. When you are faced with the temptation to tell a lie...you better run (tell the truth); when you are tempted to cheat...you better run(keep your integrity intact); when you are faced with the temptation to steal...you better run (walk away); when that hindering habit of smoking or drinking tries to creep back up on you...you better run(Don't do it!). If you're in a situation like Joseph and that old devil just won't take no for an answer...you better do like Joseph did and get some courage...if you have to run, you better run! Ruuuunnnn as if your life depended on it!!

Joseph had "promise" attached to his life. Joseph was running away from the very thing that sought to destroy him...The Enemy! You might ask the question, what does running have to do with courage? Courage simply means a quality of spirit that enables you to face danger or pain without showing fear...or the ability to manage danger. Joseph managed his temptation long enough...and when the chips were down...or when there was no one around to vouch for his character...he had to do the only thing he knew to do. I am a witness to Joseph's situation...and I did exactly what Joseph did...I literally ran from the temptation that tried to bind me up. The opposite of courage is coward. Although it would appear that Joseph was a coward by running from the woman...Joseph wasn't no fool. He knew that the eyes of God were in every place, beholding the Good and the Evil; so even if no one else was in the house, God was and he'd rather take his punishment from man, which was to later be thrown in jail because of the false accusations of Potipher's wife, than to deal with punishment from God. First Timothy 6:11 KJV says; "But thou, O man of God, flee these things; and follow after righteousness, godliness, faith, love, patience, meekness." Because of the favor that was upon Joseph's life...he continued to prosper even during his lock down season. So when resisting isn't working...you better try running!! Be Blessed.

Don't Forget the Real Reason for the Season

Every man shall give as he is able, according to the blessing of the LORD thy God which he hath given thee. – Deuteronomy 16:17, KJV

Christmas is that time of year where so many of us will be out spending more money than we earn in a week...maybe more than we earn in an entire month. There will be many who will deplete their savings account just to be able to give gifts to their loved ones...and some will give gifts to people they don't even like...just because it's Christmas. Always keep in mind that even though there are a lot of good people out shopping this time of year, there are also BAD people out "shopping" this time of year. Shopping for items they don't have to pay for...shopping for bags left uncovered in the back of someone else's vehicle...peeking into windows to see which homes are the most ripe for picking.

The television stations will begin showing movies that depict the Holiday Season...the season of fellowship...the season of Love...the season of Giving. Can you remember going to church in years past and participating in the church's Christmas play that depicted the true meaning of Christmas...or at least what the old folk used to tell us was the "Reason for the Season?" I can remember!! I can also remember that those were some of the most awesome times of my life...learning all about the birth of Jesus Christ. How He was born in the town of Bethlehem...wrapped in swaddling clothes...lying in a manger, because there was no room for Him in the Inn. The Inn Keeper had no clue as to what he was doing when he turned Joseph and Mary away, did he? How dare he not make room for the Savior! Can you imagine what the Inn Keeper must have felt like once he found out that he missed out on the opportunity to have the "Greatest Gift" ever given...born to save this world...delivered in his hotel? One thing I can say for him is this...he was very instrumental in creating the place where Jesus was born.

As you are decorating around your homes, as you are placing gifts under the tree (for those of you who will have a Christmas tree), as you are hanging lights and purchasing those tangible gifts...try to think of someone less fortunate than you. While working for one of my former employers, I was awed to find out how wonderful of a place God sent me to work for; a place whose key philanthropic mission is to "feed the hungry." Every year, a Christmas ornament is designed which displays the Coins 4 Kids logo, a map of Africa, and various other key graphics. This ornament is sold for $34 which feeds one person in Africa for an entire year. Not only did we have that medium, but cookbooks were designed and sold for $15 throughout the year and coins were collected. I've seen pictures of where the staff visited Kenya to assess the needs there and I promise you...this is truly a ministry-focused effort. We have no idea how blessed we are...I mean no idea.

If you can find just one less fortunate person to bless this year at Christmas time...take the opportunity to bless God by blessing them. I promise you that when you do this, a feeling is going to come over you like you've never felt before. It will be indescribable and overwhelming because you did something to brighten the life of someone else. When you give from your heart, you're performing one of the most exemplifying acts of love and kindness that anyone can do. I must share a short testimony that I experienced.

I used to work in Community Relations on my job and had the most awesome opportunity to go to one of our local schools, in one of the most drug and crime-ridden neighborhoods in the City of Memphis. I, along with four other colleagues were asked to participate with others from around the business community in what they called "Discovery Day" throughout the City. This program is sponsored by one of the local community agencies and is primarily focused on education and literacy. We were asked to read a special book entitled, "The Legend of Saint Nicholas" to the children. Contrary to popular belief, this Saint Nicholas we read about to the children was not the jolly old man, with the white hair and beard, wearing a red and white suede suit, with black shiny boots and belt...it was about a young boy who inherited a huge bag of gold coins from the death of his parents. Because of this, he kept it a secret.

He made friends with a young boy, who had twin sisters, who all lived with their Aunt. When Nicholas asked the little boy to come out and play ball with him, the young boy couldn't because his shoes were raggedy. One day Nicholas slipped enough coins into his pocket at school, and when the little boy found them, he went out and bought new shoes, and then was able to play with Nicholas every day. Another situation arose where the young boy shared with his new found friend Nicholas, that they didn't have beds to sleep in at their Aunt's home. Nicholas saw another opportunity to bless the little boy...so what did he do? He slipped more coins into the boy's coat pocket. Of course, the little boy took the money...went and bought a bed for himself and each of his siblings...then, he told Nicholas on another occasion that they needed another miracle; one of the twins needed glasses. Here goes Nicholas once again being a blessing to someone less fortunate than himself. To make a long story short...Nicholas was discovered when he went the last time to put the coins in the young boy's pocket, but he asked him to promise not to tell anyone. Sounds like Nicholas had the heart of Jesus...doesn't it?

The hardest part of the entire day for me was going to that school and seeing particular children who were in need. Then I realized that there was a sure fire lesson in all of that for me...and I could not write this devotional today without sharing it. Every opportunity Nicholas found to bless someone else...he did it. No one had to ask...he was in the position to get it done first hand. Not only did he hear and see the need...he met the need...NOW THAT'S MINISTRY...finding a need, and then meeting it!! Although we couldn't promote the Christmas Holiday during this time of sharing with the students... we could encourage them about "Giving." God gave the greatest gift of all times...His Son. And although we can't beat God giving... it doesn't hurt for us to try. I challenge you this Christmas to think about someone else less fortunate than you by spreading a little love and joy this Christmas Season. Adopt an Angel...or do something and give back some of what God has blessed you with this year! Be blessed.

Get Out of the Box

Behold, I will do a new thing; now it shall spring forth; shall ye not know it? I will even make a way in the wilderness, and rivers in the desert. - Isaiah 43:19 KJV

After you read this daily meditation, I want you to take a closer look at the 43rd Chapter of Isaiah. If the Word alone doesn't bless you...nothing else will. I'm encouraged to share this word with you today because it is the place where God has me in my life at this very moment. To give you a brief synopsis of Isaiah 43, God was rebuking Jacob, whose name was later changed to Israel because of his spiritual failure. What I mean by this is...he wasn't being the witness, as such; all believers are called to do once we are saved.

Did you know that it is our <u>responsibility</u> as a believer to tell others about Jesus Christ? Often in our daily walk, we get so complacent and comfortable in the place where we are, and because of that, we settle ourselves in that position not realizing that it is more harmful than helpful to us. In other words, we confine ourselves to our own little boxes (our comfort zones). We dare anyone to step within that box, and we don't have the courage to get out of the box. The box represents our paradigm...basically our mindset or way of thinking. There are two significant things about a box...the inner perimeter and the outer perimeter. When you are in the box...or let me say it like this...your comfort zone...you have your own set way of doing things. It's either my way or no way. You even determine when, where, and how God is going to show up in your situation. But do you know that our thoughts are not God's thoughts and neither are our ways His ways? Do you agree?

I want you to do this for me: imagine yourself standing inside of a box. Keep in mind, the inner perimeter of that box represents your thoughts and ways....your mindset. Now see yourself running around that box. How much room did you have to run? Where could you go? What size steps could you take? And how long did it take you to get back to the place where you started? What kind of limitations did you have? I pray that by now you've already gotten the message God is trying to get you to see. Don't stop there... imagine yourself on the outside perimeter of that box...What kind of freedom to do you have to move...to walk...to run? What about your stride...are you able to stretch out much further than you were able when you were inside of the box?

When we get outside of our own mindset...our comfort zones, and take on the mind of God...our possibilities are endless. Think about Abram, when God spoke and told him to get up and leave the place where he had built his home and was raising his family. At that time...Abram was in his comfort zone...but God asked him to "Get Out of His Box" and go to a place that I will show you. Not only did He begin to lead Abram, but because of his obedience, God made him a promise to bless him beyond measure. Abraham later became the father of many nations and a witness of the goodness of God.

I had an assignment to go and witness to a young lady on my job... and you better believe I was the first person this particular Word impacted. I have gotten comfortable in my own form of ministry on my job. I just wanted to be a light in a dark place, and use compassion where others were using harshness. When the door opened to witness, I walked away not hearing what was going on in the spirit realm. When I got back to my seat, God began to speak to me concerning what I had just done. As I left work, He continued to speak and said to me: "the reason you can't effectively witness is because you are in your comfort zone...Get out of the box!" He literally blew my mind...and so, I began to repent. Later, He began showing me how we are limited in our own way of thinking because we expect Him to work in our own way and timing. But we've got to be sensitive...having our ears tuned to the Spirit of God. Then we have to move when He says move...not when we get ready.

If you are ready to Get out of the Box, make the decision today, to change your way of thinking and allow God to take you places you wouldn't normally go yourself. Getting out of your comfort zone will cause you to be "uncomfortable," but that is what it is supposed to do. Be sensitive to the move of God...consult Him on what you've received...believe in the assignment He has given you to do...then "Get Out of the Box" when He tells you to move. God wants to do some new things through you. Remember, your blessing is tied to your obedience. Abraham was a witness to that. Be Blessed!

Don't Get It Twisted

Who is more important, the one who sits at the table or the one who serves? The one who sits at the table, of course. But not here! For I am among you as one who serves. Luke 22:27, NLT

As I began to write this devotional, I struggled with the first few lines. I didn't know whether to lead in with a rhetorical question or just say what was in my spirit to say. Well, being led of the Holy Spirit, He made my mind up for me. He said speak what I've put on your heart. For over two weeks now, the Lord has been breathing these words into me...and you will know them because they are to a song. "Sometimes I gotta remind myself that you called me, and I am at your disposal." Do these words sound familiar to anyone? For some reason, I can't shake hearing these words. No matter how many other songs I've listened to over the last couple of weeks, these words are ringing out loudly in my ears. As I write this devotion, they are ringing even more loudly.

I had to ask the question, "God, what is it that I'm not doing? Am I speaking death and not life with my tongue? Am I not building up your Kingdom? Am I not spreading the Good News? What is it God?" I began examining myself to make sure that my situation hasn't gotten me off the path to righteousness. II Corinthians 13:5 KJV tells us to, "Examine yourselves (ourselves), whether ye (we) be in the faith; prove your own selves. Know ye not your own selves, how that Jesus Christ is in you, except ye be reprobates?" I, just like a lot of other people have something going on in my life that has made me doubt whether I was a child of God. But one thing I had to remember is this: God has called me to be a disciple...to be His Ambassador...and just like Jesus went through persecution...I too will have to go through. But Jesus paved the way for me to go through this trial and not faint. Jesus set the example of what to do when all H_ _ _ has broken loose in my life. My God says in His word, "So shall they fear the name of the LORD from the west, and

61

his glory from the rising of the sun. When the enemy shall come in like a flood, the Spirit of the LORD shall lift up a standard against him." (Isaiah 59:19 KJV)

I'm not talking about high gas prices...I'm not talking about the price of milk going through the roof...I got some stuff going on that I've had to pull the Holy Anointing Oil out and sling all over my situation!! Help me up in here Holy Ghost!!! If you are reading this devotional today, do you have something going on in your life that caused you to question whether you are of God? Have you accepted a call to a special area of ministry, but yet, you aren't working it? Have you been called of God, but you're procrastinating because you feel you aren't ready to do this thing? Have you asked yourself the question, "Am I really Called, and if I am, what does that mean?" For those of us who are called, we forget what we are actually called to do. We allow distractions to cause us to miss the mark...to move away from the things God has called us to do. The reason we do this is simple, we easily forget, or might I say, we "get things twisted."

We fuss and fight over petty things, rather than hold our tongues and allow God to fight our battles. Instead of praying or seeking God about the situation, we begin looking for solutions to get even or to fix the problem ourselves. We even say that we're hearing from God, when we know that is not the case...we just heard ourselves. We do things the way we want to do them, rather than asking God for His way of doing them. Sometimes, we get so caught up in ourselves that we begin doing things that's only pleasing in our eyes. Rather than serve someone else, we hurry and sit down at the table so someone could serve us. Did you know this ain't about you? Don't get it twisted...this is all about Jesus!!

Haven't you already realized who God is...and if He allowed that present situation to take form in your life...He is able to carry you through it? I know that working in ministry can be burdensome at times...but didn't God call you to that place? Why are you fighting? Plead the Blood of Jesus over it. I got a super revelation over my situation after I began to examine myself...God showed me some things...PRAISE YOUR HIGH NAME JESUS, GLORY HALLELUJAH

TO THE KING OF KINGS AND THE LORD OF LORDS!! I found out that God had ordained it all because everything that was happening was necessary for Him to show himself in my situation. And you better know, as soon as I began to recognize this...I began to see God ALL over this thing. Every time something was done to me that was meant for evil...God used it to work for my good. So I quit fighting. Just like Joseph, everything that was done to him was meant for evil...somebody say, "BUT GOD"...He meant it for his good. I can't do anything but be thankful in my situation, because thanks is going to bring me through it and God is going to get the Glory!! So don't get it twisted, if God can do this thing for me, then He will do the same for you! Be Blessed.

Take Your Foot Off the Hose!

Scripture: **But the hour cometh, and now is, when the true worshippers shall worship the Father in spirit and in truth: for the Father seeketh such to worship Him.** – John 4:23 **But if the Spirit of Him that raised up Jesus from the dead dwell** (reside or inhabit) **in you, he that raised up Christ from the dead shall also quicken your mortal bodies by his Spirit that dwelleth in you.** – Romans 8:11 KJV

For all the born again, Holy Ghost filled, baptized believers…it's time to step up and step out! God wants to do some things through us, but we have to be willing to be used. One of the reasons we can't be used…or God jumps over many of us and chooses another person…is because we won't allow the Holy Spirit to do what He wants to do in and through us.

Walk with me for a moment and I will try to make it clear. You have to walk with me in the spirit to really hear what the spirit is saying to us. Now that you have your spiritual eyes and ears on, I want you to look at something with me. Take a water hose for instance…the purpose of the hose is to serve as a conduit or simply saying, as a guiding mechanism for water to pass through. A water hose's purpose is to guide the water from the (source) or…provider to its intended destination. Hold that thought, we will come back to the hose.

Now I want you to think about a microphone. The barrel of the microphone serves as the conduit or chamber…which holds the batteries…or shall I say the "power" that sends a transmission to the speakers, which in turn causes something else to happen.

So now we have the water hose…which holds the water and directs the water to a destination; then we have a microphone which holds the batteries…or the power which carries the sound made when a person speaks into it. Are you still with me?

Now consider a light fixture. I want you to think of a massive one...hung from the ceiling in the center of a room. Now if I used my sanctified imagination, I can see the fixture is supported by a conduit...which obviously houses the electrical wires...which carries the "power" from the source to its destination...which is the bulb sockets.

Let's go back to the water hose. If you take a hose and bend it... what do you think will happen? Exactly...it stops the flow! First Corinthians 6:19 says what? "Know ye not that your body is the temple of the Holy Ghost which is "in" you, which ye have of God, and ye are not your own?" It matters not where we are, it is our duty to sing God's praises when opportunities present themselves. Many times, we hold another person's deliverance and/or HOPE in our mouths because we refuse to be sensitive to the Holy Spirit's leading. We go to church and sit next to people who don't want to praise God, so we just sit there too. What we don't realize is...maybe that person is looking for a Holy Ghost filled, fire baptized believer in Christ to jump up and shout Hallelujah, so they can feel something too. The next time you go to the house of God and sit next to one of them sanctified, saddity saints...who don't want to praise God...tell them to "take their foot off the hose"...get up and praise God anyway. I don't care who's looking at you...I don't care who doesn't like you... don't allow your praise to be hindered. You better let go and let God have His way in you. The bible commanded us to enter into His gates with "thanksgiving" and into His courts with "praise," be thankful unto Him and bless His name, for the Lord is good...His mercy is everlasting...and His truth endures to all generations.

Hold On, It's Coming!

The LORD shall open unto thee His good treasure, the heaven to give the rain unto thy land in his season, and to bless all the work of thine hand. - Deuteronomy 28:12 KJV

Prophetic utterance for today: "You have repeatedly been urged to release the past, and I tell you truly that as soon as you let go, doors of opportunity will open wide for you to move forward in spiritual progression. Separate yourself from the emotional strain of the difficult circumstances that you have endured. Only then will you see the value of the past experiences apart from the stress, and you will know that you have gained great wisdom and insight that will serve you well in the days ahead," says the Lord.

It is my intent to write and share God's goodness with as many people as I possibly could; and oh how anxious I get when God pulls a blessing right out of the air that amazes my very intellect. But I had to wait, because God is not finished with this particular blessing. I used to write for my sister and friend, Lady LaKeisha Ford Calhoun of Memphis, TN. One particular morning, I received an email from this powerfully anointed Woman of God to write. I knew then I had to be obedient and the Lord would lead me on what to say. So as I prayed about what else I could share with the reading audience, my daily prophetic word (above) flashed before me. A very powerful woman of God at my former workplace would send them to me daily and it always met me at my point of need. I don't take credit for what the Lord says through this vessel, but I've found that as I share what the Lord says to me through her, other people are blessed as well. It seems that many of us are in the same vein with our situations and circumstances. We will never know that someone else is going through the same thing unless we share where we've been or where we are. It is important to be led of the Spirit in our time of sharing. This will keep the naysayers and the haters from knowing your business...because their intent will be to spread it before God can work it to His glory.

1 Corinthians 10:13 KJV reads: There hath no temptation taken you, but such as is common to man; but God is faithful, who will not suffer you to be tempted above that ye are able; but will within the temptation also make a way to escape, that ye may be able to bear it. In other words, no temptation or trial that comes our way is beyond the course of what others have had to face. We just have to remember that God will never let us down and He will never let us be pushed beyond the limit of what we can bear. He will always be there to help us come through it...because it's not about us...but it's about Him. He will get the glory in every one of our situations.

Either we don't know how to trust God or don't truly believe that He is mindful of us. When I first began receiving this prophetic word from the Lord through this person, I became tearful because every word spoken...every day it was spoken...was speaking directly to my situation. The more I tried to figure it out...the more clearer it became to me. God knew what it would take for me to know that it was HIM speaking and not the "person" the words were coming from. He had to use someone who knew "nothing" about my situation and circumstances to speak life into me. Many times we share what we are going through with our close friends, families, prayer partners, and sometimes co-workers...hoping they will say something that will ease our spirits, or give us a word. They may even have the answer for you...but you don't look at them in the same light as you would if your "word" came from the pulpit. Well, just imagine me sitting at my desk reading a prophetic word on my computer... instead of going in backwards...I'm falling forwards as I'm reading... holding my mouth...trying to keep the tongues from flowing...about to slobber all over my hand (Thank God for Kleenex).

Just like God came through for me, he can come through for you. All I can say is, keep your ears to the Word of God. Meditate on Him day and night. God has someone that will roll through with the very word you need that is going to speak life into your dead circumstances and situations. God is not a man that He should lie;

neither the son of man that he should repent: hath he said, and shall he not do it? or hath he spoken, and shall he not make it good? (Num 23:19 KJV) If God has made you a promise...you better believe that He will bring it to pass. He will do it in such a way that it will make your head do a double take! That's what he does to me every time he comes through with a blessing. Be blessed is my prayer for you today and hold on and be assured that whatever you need from God is on the way. Be Blessed!

His Blessings Are Unmistakable!

The blessing of the LORD, it maketh rich, and He addeth no sorrow with it. – Proverbs 10:22 KJV

My mind was turning flips as I wrote write this devotional. Although I arose this particular morning with a song of praise and worship… in the midst of my song…I could hear the words from Proverbs 10:22 KJV, as I busied myself preparing for work. I stopped singing to hear what the Lord wanted to say. I got quiet, but I heard nothing else. So what do I do? I started thinking about what He could have been trying to say when He spoke that into my spirit.

Many times when God speaks, He will speak into the atmosphere such as he did in Genesis 1 when he made heaven and earth. Because He is all powerful, all He has to do is speak and things will take form. But what happens when He speaks a word into the atmosphere? I will say that He intends for those that have an ear to hear what He speaks. When we hear Him speak, we should find solace that He is about to do something. God never speaks a word and it return unto Him void. Isaiah 55:11 KJV says and He is speaking: _"So shall my word be that goeth forth out of my mouth: it shall not return unto me void, but it shall accomplish that which I please, and it shall prosper in the thing whereto I sent it."_ Well, what is God saying? If you go back up and read verses 8 – 10 you will understand. God does not think the way we think. He doesn't work the way we work. He even declares that His thoughts are as high above the earth; therefore, the way He works surpasses the way we work, and the way He thinks goes far beyond the way we think. He then goes on further to declare that when the rain and snow descends from the sky, they do not return to the sky until they have accomplished their goal…which is to water the earth, because it is what makes things grow and blossom…**get this**…producing seed for farmers and food for the hungry. Come on somebody!!! God is getting ready to do something in His people's lives that is going to blow our minds! But don't mistake the blessing…because the enemy just might throw a false blessing in your path...be clear... God's blessings are unmistakable.

If you are reading this today, God is letting you know that He is mindful of you. He doesn't want you to forget the promise He made to you. Stop leaning to your own understanding about what you 'think' God is trying to do in your life...and just allow Him to be God! Let me repeat what He said again, "The blessing of the LORD, it maketh rich, and He addeth no sorrow with it." This was an atmosphere word today, which means not only was it for me, but He meant for it to be embraced by those who have an ear to hear what thus saith the Lord!

Let me tell you something...the first Sunday of every new year for me, you will find me in church. January 3, 2010...and I will never forget it...The devil tried to take out my child in an unfortunate situation. The FIRST Sunday of the year! Do you hear me! But MY God stepped in on our and her behalf, because there is a word over her life that SHALL come to pass...a word that will accomplish the very thing it was sent to do! Thank you, Lord! If you have gotten despondent and think that God is not going to work things out for you, I come to tell you to HOLD ON! He has some blessings that are unmistakable. Don't be deceived by what the enemy puts in your path as a so called blessing...it will be a wolf disguised as sheep. As He said in His word...His blessings maketh rich...and HE addeth no sorrow with it! And that blessing is on the way! Be Blessed!

Are You Fully Dressed

Finally, my brethren, be strong in the Lord and in the power of His might. Put on the whole armor of God, that you may be able to stand against the wiles of the devil. For we wrestle not against flesh and blood, but against principalities, against powers, against the rulers of darkness of this age, against spiritual hosts of wickedness in the heavenly places. Therefore, take up [or put on] the whole armor of God, that you may be able to withstand in the evil day, and having done all, to stand. Stand therefore, having girded your waist with truth, having put on the breastplate of righteousness, and having shod your feet with the preparation of the gospel of peace; above all, taking the shield of faith with which you are able to quench all the fiery darts of the wicked one. And take the helmet of salvation, and the sword of the Spirit, which is the Word of God; praying always with all prayer and supplication in the Spirit, being watchful to this end with all perseverance and supplication for all the saints... -Ephesians 6:10-19, NKJV

Take a good look at yourself this morning. Go ahead. That's right, take a good look at yourself from head to toe. And if you're like me, I have a mirror sitting on your desk. Do you have on shoes? I pray to the good Lord that you have on the proper amount of clothing. What about your accessories; for ladies that could be earrings, bracelets, rings. What about your make up? What about that nice tie to match your suit men of God? Many of us rush through life, but yet we spend 30 minutes, an hour or longer getting dressed in the morning whether it's to go to work, school, job interview, or an important appointment. We make sure we are fully dressed and looking out best. Our physical appearance is top notch; we're matching from head to toe.

Even though we are fully dressed in the natural; our hair is combed or brushed, there's not a hair out of place, our clothes are nicely pressed, our shoes are shined, we have on just the right amount

71

of accessories to accentuate our outfit; we look good, if we must say so ourselves, but despite how much we have on and how good we look on the outside, many of us are walking around spiritually naked, and though it's a sad commentary....we're naked and not ashamed. Consequently, the enemy is having a field day with us. We're suffering defeat on every side. We're succumbing to the wiles of the enemy, even though he's used the same trick a million times. Why? **(We're succumbing)** because we didn't take the time to get fully dressed. **(I mean dressed spiritually).**

After our morning worship service yesterday, I went out to lunch with a dear friend. After which...you know how people get once they're full...I went straight home and got in the bed. My husband had a meeting at 5:45pm so he wouldn't be there to wake me up. As he walked out of the door, I asked him to call and wake me up at 6:30pm, in just enough time to slip on my clothes and make it to the evening service at 7:00pm. Well my husband's meeting ran a little late and he was unable to call me. Thank God for the Holy Spirit because I still managed to wake up on time. But in a frenzy, I rushed to put on my clothes, then I realized I had a run in my pantyhose, so that meant I had to stop by the local store on my way; thus making me even later.

Running out of time, I left the house half dressed; flip flops and all. When I arrived at church, one could tell that I was in a rush. When asked what was wrong, I just responded, I have to go and finish getting dressed (at church). I don't know what I thought I would have missed if I had taken an extra 5-10 minutes at home and gotten fully dressed. But that would have meant I couldn't sit in my favorite seat (oh come on, you know you have one too). I would have missed the prayer and scripture (which I'm usually running around or doing something at my seat during this time anyway)...or maybe I was afraid of not having a good parking spot...because my church is notorious for starting on time (Thank God). I felt so undone because my makeup wasn't on, and I felt a little funny without my pantyhose.

Once I got myself together, hair and all, I felt like a million bucks... and I was cute too, if I must say so myself. But in the midst of service, I realized that I had forgotten something...the most important thing;

my armor. For without it, I leave myself open to the enemy; fair game, I become prey, a sitting duck, a prime target for an attack. Again, I was fully dressed in the natural, but hadn't thought about my spiritual attire at all. As cute as I was, I don't know any battles won by cuteness. I would have been a wounded or defeated "cute" soldier....when I didn't have to be. If I had just taken time to put on my armor.

In the above Scripture, Paul admonishes us to put on the whole armor of God. In other words, don't leave home half dressed. The armor of God is important because it helps us to not only fight, but it helps us to stand against the wiles [trickery and deceptions) of the enemy. As much as we hate to admit it, our fight is not against our co-workers, employer, spouse, family members, friends, church members or the person that cut you off in traffic. No ma'am. No sir. For we wrestle not against flesh and blood. What we are fighting against can't be seen with the naked eye: principalities, wicked powers, against the rulers of darkness, spiritual host in heavenly (or high) places. And guess what...having on the latest pair of Tommy Hilfiger jeans or the latest St. John suit won't help. You have to put on the whole armor...all of it.

Before you leave the house tomorrow morning, or at any time for that matter, make sure you put on the whole armor of God. Because if you don't, you will leave yourself open for the enemy's attack... and we don't need anymore wounded soldiers...especially since God has already provided everything we need to win. For the word of God promises us that if we would just put on the whole armor (belt of "truth", breastplate of "righteousness", feet shod with the preparation of the "gospel" of peace, the shield of faith (for without IT, is impossible to please God), the helmet of "salvation", and the sword of the spirit which is the "Word of God"...that we will be able to quench all the fiery darts of the wicked one. So if you are experiencing consecutive defeats, check you armor. I believe it is God's desire for us to walk in consecutive victory and if we put on the armor of God, victory shall be ours. Are you fully dressed today? If not, then take a few minutes and put on your armor. You'll be glad you did.

Bringing Things into Perspective

We are troubled on every side, yet not distressed; we are perplexed, but not in despair; Persecuted, but not forsaken; cast down, but not destroyed; Always bearing about in the body the dying of the Lord Jesus, that the life also of Jesus might be made manifest in our body. - 2 Corinthians 4:8-10, KJV

When you take a look at the above passage of scriptures, what are you feeling? What does it say to you? These are words from the BIBLE...yes words letting us know that we are going to have some rainy days, some hard times, some crying, suffering, heartache and pain...but it is how you receive these situations that determines your end result.

A pessimistic person is one who never sees the positive side of things. Not only are they negative, but they are cynical...mocking, distrustful, sarcastic...If they are in debt...they feel they will always be in debt, so they continue to incur debt without ever paying anything off. If they are sick in their body, they wear it on their face. Is your cup half empty or is it half-full? How do you see things that are happening in your life? What is your perspective on these things?

I believe many of us have been faced since the beginning of this year with some major obstacles. We've looked back over 2005 and thought we had gotten past some of those things...but they seemed to just follow us right on into this next year. You may be one of those who's considering a divorce due to your present situation, or someone who's going through a major financial battle...to the point that you are about to lose the roof over your head or your transportation... you know better than I what your trouble is. Along with all of these troubles, the enemy will begin to put things before us that may tempt us to do something outside of the Will of God.

I didn't write to prophesy a car, house, or money...but I wrote to tell you that God says in His word, "There hath no temptation taken you but such as is common to man: BUT God is faithful, who will not suffer you to be tempted above that ye are able; but will with the temptation also make a way to escape, that ye may be able to bear it." (1 Corinthians 10:13 KJV). God's word says that even though we will be faced with some trouble, we don't have to be distressed...look at the word 'distressed'. When we are distressed, we are unhappy, upset, distraught, troubled, concerned, worried, anxious or bothered. His word goes on to say that even though we may be perplexed... puzzled...at a loss...confused...Lord, how did this happen to me? I was so careful this time; we don't have to be in despair...hopeless... in misery...depressed...desolate. Even when people persecute or harass us, we are not forsaken...why? Because He said that He will never leave us nor forsake us. God is always here for us. Even when we have been cast down, just plain ole' thrown away by others, we Are not destroyed

An Optimist is a person who sees a glass half full. They are idealist or romantic...loving, passionate...tender. Optimistic people always look for the good in others because they know there is some good in everyone. An optimistic person will believe that no matter what I am going through, God is able to bring me out of it. Not only do they wait patiently for God to take them through their situation, they go through it with a smile on their face, praise on their lips, thanksgiving in their heart, and worship in their spirit. We can't forget who God is and what He is able to do. Bring the things you are going through into perspective. If you've been looking at your situation through the eyes of a pessimist...STOP! See your situation through optimistic eyes and know that it is coming to an end soon, and when it does...we will see the Glory of God magnified in your life. God Bless!

Keep Your Eyes on the Prize

Scripture: I press toward the mark for the prize of the high calling of God in Christ Jesus. – Phil 3:14 KJV

Are you tired of letting folk hold you hostage to your past? Every time you turn around, there is a constant reminder of what you use to do…who you use to do it with…where you use to go…who you went there with. Can you witness with me this morning? Did you know that your past is what actually brought you to where you are today? Believe it or not, all the things you went through…all of the things you use to do…and the people you use to do them with had purpose attached to them. Their purpose was to bring you to your expected end. Although God hasn't shown you ALL of what He has in store for you, you needed to go through what you've gone through, with whom you've gone through it with to get you to where you are today. Yes, you might feel sorry about the past, but you do not have to be held hostage to it.

Many of us have done things we are ashamed of, and some may even be living in the tension or stressing over some skeletons in the closest that you fear may come back to haunt you later. I'm here to tell you that you don't have to fear that mess from the past any longer, because our hope is in Christ. You can let go of past guilt and look forward to what Jesus will help us to become. Think about this for a moment. Dwelling or thinking on the past is likened to looking in a rear-view mirror. The mirror might tell you that objects in the mirror are larger than they appear, but the fact yet remains that those things are behind you and eventually will become tiny specks as you continue to go forward…as you continue to PRESS. Are you with me? Now your future is likened to looking through the front window of the vehicle. As you are PRESSING your way forward into your future, you begin to see things you've never seen before. You begin to gain new experiences…new relationships…and a greater perspective on life. Those things you are coming to are much larger than those things behind you. Are you ready for the things that God has in store for you up ahead? I know I am, and I am not letting no devil in hell keep me from getting what God has for me.

One thing you should always keep in mind; the size of the rear-view mirror (your past) cannot compare to the size of your front window (your future). What are you saying Evangelist Israel? What I'm trying to tell you is that the sufferings of our present time (or the past) are not worthy to be compared to the Glory (your future) that shall be revealed in us. Your latter shall be greater!! What's ahead of you is much greater than what you've gotten behind you. I'm here to let you know that as long as you keep looking into that rear view mirror, you will never be delivered...you will never defeat the enemy...you will never walk in victory. You've got to look at what's ahead. Paul says it like this, "I press (lay hold, apprehend, capture) toward the mark (the finish line) for the prize (the goal, the purpose for which I live, the object of my salvation) of the high calling in Christ Jesus."

Stop dwelling on your past. Begin to concentrate on your relationship with God and how you can please Him more and more with your life. If you've repented, you've been forgiven of all of your sins. You just need to move on to a life of faith and obedience. You have a fuller and more meaningful life ahead of you because of your hope in Jesus Christ. I encourage you today to keep your eyes on the prize, which is Christ Jesus, as you continue to PRESS in your daily walk with Him. Be blessed is my prayer for you on today.

<u>Overcoming the Spirit of Ungratefulness</u>

Scripture: I know how to be abased, and I know how to abound; everywhere and in all things I am instructed both to be full and to be hungry, both to abound and to suffer need. - Philippians 4:12, KJV

I wonder how long it took Paul to get to this place...the place of contentment. I don't know about you, but I'm not sure if this is an area that I can truly perfect...and although I may never be able to perfect it, I can say that I have come a long way and now know what contentment means. I guess you could say that I have grown up...I'm no longer drinking milk...but I'm able to chew some meat now.

I can remember so vividly one Sunday night at church, we were asked for a sacrificial seed offering of $10.00. I had only $16.00 to carry me through the entire week. I gave the $10 and just believed that God would take care of my needs for the week. When the end of the week had come, I had the same $6 dollars in my wallet that I started the week with. Every day of that week, God had a ram in a bush for me. One day I went to the cafeteria to buy lunch and as I got ready to pay for it, the lady at the register told me..."put your money back in your purse"...you are covered. Then several days that week, I was asked out to lunch by co-workers who paid the tab, and on one final note...I had a Board Meeting to attend and was told to come to the luncheon afterwards. So you see, when we walk in obedience to God's Word, He will take care of our needs. We are encouraged in the Word to not worry, especially about tomorrow. Matthew 6:34 KJV reads, "Take therefore no thought for the morrow: for the morrow shall take thought for the things of itself." Don't you know that if God blesses you to get through one day, He can bless you to get through the next? If we just live one day at a time (which is all we really have)...we can avoid being consumed with worry.

The reason Paul was content is because he could see life from God's point of view. Paul focused on what he was supposed to do and not on what he felt he should have as possessions. One particular Sunday, my pastor sung a song titled "I Won't Complain." As he was singing this song, I began thinking about all the recent complaints I had been making, such as not having anything to wear to work. I have a decent size closet packed with dresses, suits, pants, skirts, blouses, sweaters, shoes, boots, scarves, purses (see where I'm going). I began to cry. Why? Because how could I complain about not having anything to wear, when in fact I never wore the same thing twice in a two to three-week time period. Just a short while ago, I had so many clothes that I had to give an entire wardrobe away, and here I am complaining about not having anything to wear to work. What I really wanted was something "new" to wear. Then I began to think about the people who don't have a change of clothes at all…people with no shoes to wear…no food to eat…no roof over their heads and I had to repent.

Don't get me wrong, I am ever so grateful for the things that God has given me…but I just had a relapse…forgot or didn't realize that I was complaining. I told you that I haven't perfected this thing yet. We all have to get to the place where we become grateful for whatever God has given us. If we recognize that there is someone out there with a lot less than what we have, then appreciation can be realized and we won't harvest the attitude of ungratefulness. When I first started dealing with ungratefulness, I was living in a much smaller home. Although I was grateful for having a roof over my head, I had a relapse…I found myself complaining because I wanted more room. Once I realized that I was in the state of complaining again, I had to repent and ask for forgiveness, because I remembered that there are people in this world who are homeless. Some live in shelters, while others live on the street…whether by choice or by force, they are yet homeless. So I began to tell God "Thank You" for my home because at least I have one. There were times when I looked into the freezer and said that I didn't have anything to cook for dinner. Well, I didn't say there wasn't anything in there to cook…I just didn't want what I had. Did I forget about the people standing in the soup-line waiting on a hot bowl of soup and a piece of bread, just to get a meal for the day? I guarantee you…those people have a greater appreciation for what they are able to get than those of us who have more. I've realized that contentment is necessary. Paul concentrated on eternal things, not laying his treasures on earth. Where do your perspectives lie? What about your priorities? Are you grateful for what you have and where you are? Are you complaining because you don't have everything that you want?

Even when we are going through the storm and the rain, we are to be grateful for where God has us, because He promises that trouble won't last always. We know that if He allowed us to enter into the valley, then He can surely deliver us from our valley experiences. If He allows us to be in the midst of the storm, then surely He can give us peace in that storm. But we must show Him that we are grateful for where we are because we know that He can deliver us. How do you overcome the spirit of ungratefulness? Just remember where you are....where He's brought you from...and where you could be if it wasn't for His grace and mercy. In other words, all you need is a memory. Be blessed.

Stay on the Wheel

Jeremiah 1:5 "Before I formed thee in the belly, I knew thee; and before thou camest forth out of the womb I sanctified thee; and I ordained thee a prophet unto the nations."-Background - Jeremiah 18:1-6 KJV

The story of Jeremiah's calling is a powerful example of how God chooses certain individuals who possess the character he is looking for, to do a particular job. Jeremiah had a bold calling on his life. It was to call a nation to repentance. And just like God chose Jeremiah, He has chosen some of us to do powerful things on this earth for the Kingdom. Our problem is that we don't realize the character we possess or we won't stay in his Will (on the wheel) long enough for that character to be developed.

In our background scripture, God woke Jeremiah out of his sleep and told him to go down to the Potter's house and when he got there he had something for him to see (and I'm paraphrasing here). Jeremiah didn't question what God told him to do, unlike us. When God tells us to pray for our enemy, that is what he means for us to do because that may be where our deliverance lies. But we question God...God, why do I have to pray for my enemy, they don't like me anyway...God why, why, why?

There are three things we need to understand from this text: (1) The purpose of the Potter - The Potter(God) decides the clay's(our) purpose before it goes onto the wheel and he also decides what "qualities or character" this piece of clay needs to serve its intended "purpose". If you've ever seen a potter work with a piece of clay, then you know that in order for the clay to take its intended form, the potter never takes his hands off of the clay while 'it is on the wheel'.

(2) The purpose of the clay(us) - because the potter has already determined what the piece of clay will be when it is put on the

wheel, it is the clays' purpose to 'yield' to the direction of the potter's hands. Jer. 18:4 tells us that the vessel was marred while in the hand of the potter, so he made it again. The word "mar" means damaged, hurt, disrupt. Yes, there will be times when we endure hardship, heartache, and pain while in the hands of the Potter, but Heb. 13:5 KJV say *"He will never leave us nor forsake us"*. It is at this point that if we yield to the Potter's hands he can make us whole again.

(3) The purpose of the wheel - the wheel controls the speed at which the potter turns the clay and has to be controlled by the Potter. The potter doesn't stop the wheel until it is time to take the vessel off. This is why it is so important for us to "Stay on the Wheel", because as long as we are on the wheel, we remain in His Will. If we stay on the wheel, God has the power to mold and make us the way he desires us to be. It is on the wheel where he can strip us of all impurities and make us clean vessels again.

*Stay on the Wheel was the opening devotional for Volume I and I thought it befitting to close out Volume II with it. As children of Christ, we are made in God's image…and at the same time, we each have been given distinct character traits. God knows us by name, because he knew us before he formed us in the bellies of our parents. Let's remember that God is not taken by surprise with anything that happens in the lives of his children. He is mindful of you and He is there for you at all times. Be faithful over a few things and watch him grant you more to rule over!

Printed in the United States
by Baker & Taylor Publisher Services